Broadway Musicals

Show by Show

1960-1971

Contents

3 Foreword
3 About The Author Of The Text
4 About The Shows
80 As Long As He Needs Me
162 Being Alive
177 Broadway Baby
60 Brotherhood Of Man
132 Cabaret
31 Camelot
82 Consider Yourself
174 Day By Day
112 Do I Hear A Waltz?
73 Gonna Build A Mountain
115 Half A Sixpence
151 Happy Time, The
106 Hello, Dolly!
55 I Ain't Down Yet
57 I Believe In You
180 I Don't Know How To Love Him
67 I've Got Your Number
37 If Ever I Would Leave You
138 If He Walked Into My Life
89 If I Were A Rich Man
109 It Only Takes A Moment
40 Make Someone Happy
142 Mame
97 Matchmaker
62 Milk And Honey
147 My Cup Runneth Over
48 Never Will I Marry
123 Nothing Can Stop Me Now!
119 On A Clear Day (You Can See Forever)
75 Once In A Lifetime
53 Our Language Of Love
85 People
70 Real Live Girl
43 Soon It's Gonna Rain
103 Sunrise, Sunset
184 Superstar
64 Sweetest Sounds, The
46 Try To Remember
145 We Need A Little Christmas
121 What Did I Have That I Don't Have?
78 What Kind Of Fool Am I?
126 Who Can I Turn To
188 Who Is Silvia?
135 Willkommen
129 Wonderful Day Like Today, A
165 You Could Drive A Person Crazy
155 Zorba Theme (Life Is)

Hal Leonard Publishing Corporation
7777 West Bluemound Road P.O. Box 13819 Milwaukee, WI 53213

ISBN 0-7935-0808-8

Foreword

The Broadway musical, with its combination of music, dancing and visual delights, is truly one of America's great cultural treasures. From the hundreds of productions which have been mounted since 1891, we've selected the best music, and combined it with interesting facts and photographs to create a one-of-a-kind seven-volume songbook series: Broadway Musicals - Show By Show.

About The Author Of The Text

The comments about each show in this collection are excerpted from the book *Broadway Musicals Show by Show* by author Stanley Green. Mr. Green (1923-1990) was highly regarded as one of the leading scholars in the field of musical theatre. His eleven books are among the most widely read on the subject, including *The World of Musical Comedy, The Rodgers and Hammerstein Story, Broadway Musicals of the 30s, Starring Fred Astaire, Encyclopaedia of the Musical Theatre, Encyclopaedia of the Musical Film, The Great Clowns of Broadway, Broadway Musicals Show by Show,* and *Hollywood Musicals Year by Year.* He also compiled and edited *The Rodgers and Hammerstein Fact Book,* the definitive reference on that phenomenally successful collaboration.

Mr. Green was born in New York and lived there throughout his life. He began his writing career as a record reviewer for *Saturday Review,* and later was a contributing editor for *HiFi/Stereo Review.* His articles appeared regularly in such publications as *The New York Times, Musical America, Variety,* and *The Atlantic Monthly.* He worked as a film publicist in New York and London, and was public relations advisor to ASCAP for the years 1961-1965. In 1967 he wrote the script for the revue *Salute to the American Musical Theatre,* first performed at the Waldorf-Astoria, and subsequently presented at the White House on three consecutive evenings. He also wrote the script for "The Music of Kurt Weill" and was music advisor for "Review of Reviews," two programs presented at Lincoln Center in New York.

In 1974, at the request of Richard Rodgers, Mr. Green appeared with the composer on the first videotaped program for the Theatre Collection of the New York Public Library at Lincoln Center. He has been involved with many recording projects, including a 100-record series on Broadway musicals for the Franklin Mint, and the album *Starring Fred Astaire,* which he co-produced for Columbia. In 1987 he moderated a series of seminars marking the 100th birthday of George Abbott. Mr. Green presented many lectures on musical theatre and film at Union College, University of Hartford, New York University, C. W. Post College, Lincoln Center Library, Goodspeed Opera, and Marymount College. He continued to be active as a writer and researcher until the time of his death in December of 1990.

CAMELOT

Music:
Frederick Loewe

Lyrics & book:
Alan Jay Lerner

Producers:
Alan Jay Lerner, Frederick Loewe & Moss Hart

Director:
Moss Hart (Alan Jay Lerner uncredited)

Choreographer:
Hanya Holm

Cast:
**Richard Burton,
Julie Andrews,
Roddy McDowall,
Robert Coote,
Robert Goulet,
M'el Dowd,
John Cullum,
Bruce Yarnell,
David Hurst,
Michael Kermoyan**

Songs:
**"I Wonder What the King Is Doing Tonight";
"The Simple Joys of Maidenhood";
"Camelot";
"Follow Me";
"C'est Moi";
"The Lusty Month of May";
"Then You May Take Me to the Fair";
"How to Handle a Woman";
"Before I Gaze at You Again";
"If Ever I Would Leave You";
"What Do the Simple Folk Do?";
"Fie On Goodness!";
"I Loved You Once in Silence";
"Guenevere"**

New York run:
Majestic Theatre, December 3, 1960; 873 p.

Camelot. Julie Andrews leading the courtiers in "The Lusty Month of May." (Friedman-Abeles)

Lerner and Loewe's first Broadway undertaking following their spectacular success, *My Fair Lady,* was based on T.H. White's retelling of the Arthurian legend, *The Once and Future King.* Originally titled *Jenny Kissed Me, Camelot* reunited the composer and lyricist with director Moss Hart (who joined Lerner and Loewe as co-producer), fair lady Julie Andrews, Col. Blimpish actor Robert Coote, choreographer Hanya Holm, scene designer Oliver Smith, music director Franz Allers, and orchestrators Robert Russell Bennett and Philip J. Lang. During the tryout, Moss Hart (who died a year later) was hospitalized with a heart attack and Lerner temporarily took over as director. The show had the biggest advance sale in Broadway history up to that time.

The opulently mounted production was a somewhat somber affair that dealt with the chivalrous Knights of the Round Table and the tragic romantic triangle involving noble King Arthur (Richard Burton), his errant Queen Guenevere (Julie Andrews), and Arthur's trusted Sir Lancelot du Lac (Robert Goulet). At the end, with his kingdom in ruins and his wife with another man, the King can still urge a young boy to tell everyone the story "that once there was a fleeting wisp of glory call Camelot." The touring company, which traveled for a year and a half, had a cast headed by William Squire (Arthur), Kathryn Grayson (Guenevere), Robert Peterson (Lancelot), Jan Moody (Morgan Le Fay), and Arthur Treacher (King Pellinore).

Camelot. Julie Andrews and Richard Burton. (Friedman-Abeles)

In 1980, Richard Burton recreated his original role in a touring revival that played a limited New York engagement in July. Christine Ebersole played Guenevere and Richard Muenz was Lancelot. Because of ill health, Burton was succeeded on the road by Richard Harris who also came back briefly to New York — in November 1981 — with Meg Bussert now playing the queen. In all, this company toured for almost three years. Harris had previously played King Arthur in the 1967 film version, which also starred Vanessa Redgrave (Guenevere) and Franco Nero (Lancelot).

A previous — and far more lighthearted — view of King Arthur's court was found in Rodgers and Hart's 1927 hit, *A Connecticut Yankee.*

GREENWILLOW

Music & lyrics:
Frank Loesser

Book:
Lesser Samuels & Frank Loesser

Producer:
Robert Willey

Director:
George Roy Hill

Choreographer:
Joe Layton

Cast:
Anthony Perkins, Cecil Kelloway, Pert Kelton, Ellen McCown, William Chapman, Grover Dale

Songs:
"A Day Borrowed from Heaven"; "The Music of Home"; "Gideon Briggs, I Love You"; "Summertime Love"; "Walking Away Whistling"; "Never Will I Marry"; "Faraway Boy"

New York run:
Alvin Theatre, March 8, 1960; 95 p.

B.J. Chute's novel was turned into a homespun fantasy that had to do with quaint superstitions and folklore of a mythical village located on the Meander River — or somewhere down the road from Brigadoon and Glocca Morra. The whimsical tale takes up the conflict of young Gideon Briggs (Anthony Perkins) who would like nothing better than to remain at home and marry his summertime love, Dorrie (Ellen McCown), but who fears that the curse of his family's "call to wander solitary" will someday make him run off to sail distant seas. Though tarrying on Broadway only three months, *Greenwillow* has long been admired for the airy, otherworldly charms of Frank Loesser's atypical score. The production also marked Anthony Perkins' first — and so far only — Broadway musical.

Do Re Mi

Music:
Jule Styne

Lyrics:
Betty Comden & Adolph Green

Book:
Garson Kanin

Producer:
David Merrick

Director:
Garson Kanin

Choreographers:
Marc Breaux & DeeDee Wood

Cast:
Phil Silvers,
Nancy Walker,
John Reardon,
David Burns,
George Mathews,
George Givot,
Nancy Dussault

Songs:
"It's Legitimate";
"I Know About Love";
"Cry Like the Wind";
"Fireworks";
"What's New at the Zoo?";
"The Late Late Show";
"Adventure";
"Make Someone Happy"

New York run:
St. James Theatre, December 26, 1960; 400 p.

Do Re Mi. "It's Legitimate" sing Phil Silvers, George Mathews, George Givot, and David Burns. (Friedman-Abeles)

A raucous satire on the music business — with special emphasis on the jukebox industry — *Do Re Mi* was full of characters reminiscent of the raffish denizens of *Guys and Dolls.* It was particularly blessed by offering two outstanding clowns in Phil Silvers as the pushiest of patsies and Nancy Walker as his long-suffering spouse. The story, which Garson Kanin adapted from his own novel, concerns Hubie Cram, a would-be bigshot, who induces three retired slot-machine mobsters (David Burns, George Mathews, and George Givot) to muscle in on the jukebox racket. Though this does not make him the fawned-upon tycoon he has always dreamed of becoming, Hubie does succeed in turning a waitress (Nancy Dussault) into a singing star. He also shows his musical knowledge by instructing a group of studio musicians on how each one is to play his instrument. His modest comment: "You hang around, you learn."

THE FANTASTICKS

Music:
Harvey Schmidt

Lyrics & book:
Tom Jones

Producer:
Lore Noto

Director:
Word Baker

Cast:
Jerry Orbach, Rita Gardner, Kenneth Nelson, William Larson, Hugh Thomas, Tom Jones, George Curley, Richard Stauffer

Songs:
"Try to Remember"; "Much More"; "It Depends on What You Pay"; "Soon It's Gonna Rain"; "I Can See It"; "Plant a Radish"; "Round and Round"; "They Were You"

New York run:
Sullivan Street Playhouse, May 3, 1960; (still running 11/1/89)

The Fantasticks. Jerry Orbach, Rita Gardner, and Kenneth Nelson. (Friedman-Abeles)

The statistics alone are, well, fantastic. No other New York stage production has ever played so many performances (over 12,280 as of November 1, 1989) and there is still no end in sight. Moreover, by the time of the show's 27th year at the 150-seat Greenwich Village theatre, there had been over 10,000 productions throughout the World, of which some 500 were performed in more than 66 foreign countries. There have also been 15 national touring companies. As for profits, the original backers have so far received a return of over 9,620% on their initial investment of $16,500. Curiously, the original critical reception was not encouraging and producer Lore Noto seriously considered closing the show after its first week. But an Off-Broadway award, the popularity of the song "Try to Remember," and, most important, word of mouth, all helped turn the musical's fortunes around.

The whimsical fantasy is concerned with the theme of seasonal rebirth — or the paradox of "why Spring is born out of Winter's laboring pains." The tale, freely adapted from Edmond Rostand's 1894 play, *Les Romanesques,* is told with a cast of eight and performed on a platform with a minimum of props. The neighboring fathers (Hugh Thomas and William Larsen) of Luisa and Matt (Rita Gardner and Kenneth Nelson), though good friends, feel they must appear as enemies to make sure that their progenies fall in love. Having thought up this bit of logic they next find a way to reverse themselves by hiring El Gallo (Jerry Orbach), aided by The Old Actor (Tom Jones) and The Indian (George Curley), to perform a mock rape by moonlight so that Matt might prove his valor, thus paving the way for a reconciliation. But daylight reveals the parental deception, the lovers quarrel, and the young man goes off to see the world. After a number of degrading experiences, he returns home to Luisa's waiting arms firm in the knowledge that "without a hurt the heart is hollow."

To date, the New York company has had over 34 El Gallos (including Bert Convy, David Cryer, and Keith Charles), over 32 Luisas (including Eileen Fulton, Betsy Joslyn, Kathryn Morath, and Judy Blazer), and over 26 Matts (including Craig Carnelia and Bruce Cryer). F. Murray Abraham played The Old Actor in 1967, and producer Lore Noto played the Boy's Father from 1970 to 1986.

Harvey Schmidt and Tom Jones had originally written the musical under the title *Joy Comes to Dead Horse,* in which the characters were Mexican and Anglo families living on adjoining ranches in the American Southwest. Dissatisfied with the overblown concept, they cut the story down to one act, reduced the number of characters, and retitled the show *The Fantasticks.* It was staged in this fashion at Barnard College in the summer of 1959. Lore Noto saw it there, and at his urging Schmidt and Jones rewrote it once again, this time as an intimate two-act musical.

Irma La Douce

Music:
Marguerite Monnot

Lyrics & book:
Julian More, David Heneker & Monty Norman

Producer:
David Merrick

Director:
Peter Brook

Choreographer:
Onna White

Cast:
Elizabeth Seal, Keith Michell, Clive Revill, George S. Irving, Stuart Damon, Fred Gwynne, Elliott Gould

Songs:
"The Bridge of Caulaincourt"; "Our Language of Love"; "Dis-Donc"; "Irma la Douce"; "There Is Only One Paris for That"

New York run:
Plymouth Theatre, September 29, 1960; 524 p.

Irma la Douce. The main performers in the scene are Keith Michell, Elizabeth Seal, and Clive Revill. (Friedman-Abeles)

Broadway's first hit with music by a French composer, *Irma la Douce* originated in Paris in 1956 with book and lyrics by Alexandre Breffort and ran for four years. The English-language adaptation opened two years later in London and gave 1,512 performances. With Elizabeth Seal, Keith Michell, and Clive Revill recreating their roles in New York — Miss Seal was the only female member of the cast — the production at the Plymouth Theatre (on 45th Street west of Broadway) was a virtual carbon of the West End original. In the story, Irma is a pure-at-heart Parisian prostitute and Nestor (Mr. Michell) is a poor student who is anxious to have Irma all for his own. The student gets the idea to disguise himself as an aged benefactor named Oscar who supposedly has enough money to be the lady's only patron. Nestor, however, grows jealous of Irma's affection for Oscar and "kills" him. He is sent to Devil's Island, but manages to escape, prove his innocence, and return to his beloved. All the songs — including the chief ballad, "Our Language of Love" — were cut from the 1963 film version starring Shirley MacLaine and Jack Lemmon.

THE UNSINKABLE MOLLY BROWN

Music & lyrics:
Meredith Willson

Book:
Richard Morris

Producers:
Theatre Guild & Dore Schary

Director:
Dore Schary

Choreographer:
Peter Gennaro

Cast:
Tammy Grimes, Harve Presnell, Cameron Prud'homme, Mony Dalmes, Edith Meiser, Mitchell Gregg, Christopher Hewett

Songs:
"I Ain't Down Yet"; "Belly Up to the Bar, Boys"; "Colorado, My Home"; "I'll Never Say No to You"; "My Own Brass Bed"; "Are You Sure?"; "Dolce Far Niente"

New York run:
Winter Garden, November 3, 1960; 532 p.

The Unsinkable Molly Brown. Tammy Grimes and Harve Presnell. (Friedman-Abeles)

Providing Tammy Grimes with her most rewarding role in a musical, *The Unsinkable Molly Brown* retold the saga of a near-legendary figure of the Colorado silver mines who rose from a poverty-stricken background in Hannibal, Missouri, through her spunky determination to be "up where the people are," and by having the good fortune to marry a lucky prospector, "Leadville Johnny" Brown (Harve Presnell). After failing to crash Denver society, Molly drags Johnny off to Europe where despite her gaucheries, or because of them, she becomes a social leader in Monte Carlo. Molly almost loses Johnny, but following her heroism displayed during the sinking of the *Titanic,* she wins back her husband and wins over the elite of Denver. The score Meredith Willson turned out was much in the same Americana vein as *The Music Man,* complete with breezy marches, rugged male choruses, back country dance numbers, and revivalistic exhortations. The movie version came out in 1964 with Debbie Reynolds as Molly and Presnell again as Johnny.

HOW TO SUCCEED IN BUSINESS WITHOUT REALLY TRYING

Music & lyrics:
Frank Loesser

Book:
Abe Burrows

Producers:
Cy Feuer & Ernest Martin

Director:
Abe Burrows

Choreographers:
Bob Fosse, Hugh Lambert

Cast:
Robert Morse, Rudy Vallee, Bonnie Scott, Virginia Martin, Charles Nelson Reilly, Ruth Kobart, Sammy Smith, Donna McKechnie

Songs:
"Coffee Break"; "The Company Way"; "A Secretary Is Not a Toy"; "Grand Old Ivy"; "Paris Original"; "Rosemary"; "I Believe in You"; "Brotherhood of Man"

New York run:
46th Street Theatre, October 14, 1961; 1,417 p.

How To Succeed in Business Without Really Trying. Robert Morse and Bonnie Scott. (Friedman-Abeles)

The program credit for *How to Succeed in Business Without Really Trying* indicates that the musical was based on Shepherd Mead's tongue-in-cheek manual, but since the book had no plot Abe Burrows' script was actually based on an unproduced play by Jack Weinstock and Willie Gilbert (whose program credit, also incorrect, indicates that they were co-librettists). That play had been sent to producers Cy Feuer and Ernest Martin who then enlisted Burrows and Frank Loesser, their *Guys and Dolls* team, to turn it into a musical comedy. Bob Fosse was brought in during rehearsals to take charge of the musical staging.

In the sassy sendup of the Horatio Alger myth, our disarmingly boyish hero J. Pierpont Finch (Robert Morse) owes his advancement — from window washer to Chairman of the Board of the World Wide Wicket Company — not to hard work but to his ability to make others work hard for him. As it traces Finch's step-by-step back-stabbing way up the corporate ladder, the show skewers such aspects of Big Business as nepotism, old-school ties, the coffee break, the office party, the sycophantic yes-men, the executive washroom (where Finch serenades his image in the mirror with the worshipful "I Believe in You"), and the boardroom presentation. The musical became the fourth to win the Pulitzer Prize for drama. Robert Morse and Rudy Vallee, who played J.B. Biggley, the stuffy president of the company, were also in the 1967 movie.

MILK AND HONEY

Music & lyrics:
Jerry Herman

Book:
Don Appell

Producer:
Gerald Oestreicher

Director:
Albert Marre

Choreographer:
Donald Saddler

Cast:
Robert Weede, Mimi Benzell, Molly Picon, Tommy Rall, Lanna Saunders, Juki Arkin

Songs:
"Shalom"; "Milk and Honey"; "There's No Reason in the World"; "That Was Yesterday"; "Let's Not Waste A Moment"; "Like A young Man"; "As Simple As That"

New York run:
Martin Beck Theatre, October 10, 1961, 543 p.

For his initial Broadway assignment, composer-lyricist Jerry Herman joined playwright Don Appell to create the first musical with an Israeli setting. After spending some weeks in Israel, the writers agreed on a story concerning American tourists so that the score would not have to be written entirely in a minor key. *Milk and Honey* (originally titled *Shalom)* was primarily about a romance that blooms in a desert *moshav* between a middle-aged man separated from his wife (Robert Weede) and an almost middle-aged widow (Mimi Benzell). Though Phil would like Ruth to remain with him, she is unhappy about an extended non-matrimonial relationship, and — when last seen — Phil is on his way to make one final appeal for a divorce. Comic relief was provided by Molly Picon (a star of the Yiddish theatre in her only Broadway musical) as a husband-hunting widow.

STOP THE WORLD — I WANT TO GET OFF

Music, lyrics & book:
Leslie Bricusse & Anthony Newley

Producer:
David Merrick

Director:
Anthony Newley

Choreographers:
Virginia Mason, John Broome

Cast:
Anthony Newley, Anna Quayle, Jennifer Baker, Susan Baker

Songs:
"Typically English";
"Gonna Build a Mountain";
"Once in a Lifetime";
"Someone Nice Like You";
"What Kind Of Fool Am I?"

New York run:
Shubert Theatre, October 3, 1962; 555 p.

A hit in London a year before it was presented in New York, *Stop the World — I Want to Get Off* unveiled the multiple talents of the British team of Leslie Bricusse and Anthony Newley. Newley starred in the musical, in which he played Littlechap, and the allegorical tale had much to say about man's drive for fame and power and the disillusionment that sets in once these goals are attained. (Rodgers and Hammerstein had previously dealt with the same general theme in *Allegro.)* In a setting designed by Sean Kenny to resemble a circus tent, Littlechap — wearing white-face clown makeup — rises in the world of business and politics after marrying the boss's daughter (Anna Quayle). Not above a little philandering with Russian, German, and American girls (all played by Miss Quayle), Littlechap ends his days ruminating — in "What Kind of Fool Am I?" — about his misspent life. Newley was succeeded during the run by Joel Grey, and his part in the 1966 movie was played by Tony Tanner. A revised adaptation came back to Broadway in 1978 with Sammy Davis Jr. Davis also did a film version of this version under the modest rubric *Sammy Stops the World.*

NO STRINGS

Music & lyrics:
Richard Rodgers

Book:
Samuel Taylor

Producer:
Richard Rodgers

Director-choreographer:
Joe Layton

Cast:
Richard Kiley, Diahann Carroll, Polly Rowles, Noelle Adam, Bernice Massi, Don Chastain, Alvin Epstein, Mitchell Gregg

Songs:
"The Sweetest Sounds"; "Loads of Love"; "La La La"; "Nobody Told Me"; "Look No Further"; "Maine"; "No Strings"

New York run:
54th Street Theatre, March 15, 1962; 580 p.

No Strings. Diahann Carroll and Richard Kiley. (Friedman-Abeles)

One appearance on the Jack Paar television show was all it took for Diahann Carroll to convince Richard Rodgers that she should be starred on Broadway in a Richard Rodgers musical. *No Strings,* the musical that resulted, was Rodgers' first production after the death of his partner, Oscar Hammerstein II, and the only one for which the composer also supplied his own lyrics. The work proved to be highly innovative in a number of ways: it placed the orchestra backstage, it put musicians onstage to accompany singers, it had the principals and chorus move scenery and props in full view of the audience, and — conforming to the show's title — it removed the string section from the orchestra. In addition, it was concerned with an interracial love affair, though the matter of race was never discussed. The leading characters were Barbara Woodruff (Miss Carroll), a high fashion model living in Paris, and David Jordan (Richard Kiley), a former Pulitzer Prize-winning novelist now a sponging "Europe bum." After meeting they enjoy hearing the sweetest sounds in such romantic surroundings as Monte Carlo, Honfleur, Deauville, and St. Tropez. The story ends, with no strings attached, as the writer returns home alone to Maine to try to resume his career. During the run, Kiley and Miss Carroll were succeeded by Howard Keel and Barbara McNair, who then toured. The 54th Street Theatre, formerly the Adelphi, was renamed the George Abbott before it was demolished.

Little Me

Music:
Cy Coleman

Lyrics:
Carolyn Leigh

Book:
Neil Simon

Producers:
Cy Feuer & Ernest Martin

Directors:
Cy Feuer & Bob Fosse

Choreographer:
Bob Fosse

Cast:
Sid Caesar, Virginia Martin, Nancy Andrews, Mort Marshall, Joey Faye, Swen Swenson, Peter Turgeon, Mickey Deems, Gretchen Cryer

Songs:
"The Other Side of the Tracks"; "I Love You"; "Be a Performer"; "Boom-Boom"; "I've Got Your Number"; "Real Live Girl"; "Poor Little Hollywood Star"; "Here's to Us"

New York run:
Lunt-Fontanne Theatre, November 17, 1962; 257 p.

Little Me. Sid Caesar (as Amos Pinchley) and Virginia Martin. (Friedman-Abeles)

Although Neil Simon's wickedly funny, outlandishly plotted libretto for *Little Me* was based on Patrick Dennis' novel about the rise of a voluptuous beauty from Drifters' Row, Venezuela, Illinois, to a Southampton estate, it was written primarily to show off the protean comic gifts of Sid Caesar playing all seven of the men who figured prominently in our heroine's life. Chief among the Caesar characterizations was Noble Eggleston, the over-achieving snob who loves poor Belle Schlumpfert as much as he is able ("considering you're riffraff and I am well-to-do"), studies medicine and law at Harvard and Yale, becomes a flying ace in World War I, wins election as governor of both North and South Dakota, and, eventually, is the man with whom Belle literally walks into the sunset. The actor was also seen as Amos Pinchley, an 88-year-old miserly banker; Val du Val, a flashy French entertainer; Fred Poitrine, the hick soldier who marries Belle and quickly expires; Otto Schnitzler, a dictatorial Hollywood director; Prince Cherney, the lachrymose impoverished ruler of the duchy of Rosenzweig; and Noble Jr., an over-achieving chip who studies both at Juilliard and Georgia Tech to become a musical engineer. Highlights of the score were the wistful "Real Live Girl," sung by World War I doughboys, and the sassy, seductive "I've Got Your Number," sung and danced by Swen Swenson, as Belle's faithful admirer.

In 1982, a revised version of *Little Me* — with James Coco, Victor Garber and Mary Gordon Murray — had a disappointingly short run on Broadway.

OLIVER!

Music, lyrics & book:
Lionel Bart

Producers:
David Merrick & Donald Albery

Director:
Peter Cole

Cast:
Clive Revill, Georgia Brown, Bruce Prochnik, Willoughby Goddard, Hope Jackman, Danny Sewell, David Jones, Geoffrey Lumb

Songs:
"Food Glorious Food"; "Where Is Love?"; "Consider Yourself"; "You've Got to Pick a Pocket or Two"; "It's a Fine Life"; "Oom-Pah-Pah"; "I'd Do Anything"; "As Long as He Needs Me"; "Who Will Buy?"; "Reviewing the Situation"

New York run:
Imperial Theatre, January 6, 1963; 774 p.

Oliver! Georgia Brown, David Jones, Bruce Prochnik, and Clive Revill in the "I'd Do Anything" number. (Friedman-Abeles)

Lionel Bart's *Oliver!,* which opened in London in 1960, held the West End longrun record for a musical until overtaken by *Jesus Christ Superstar,* and its Broadway facsimilie — also directed by Peter Cole and designed by Sean Kenny — was the longest running musical import until overtaken by *Evita.* Adapted from Charles Dickens' *Oliver Twist,* the stage version offered a somewhat jollied up view of the ordeal of an orphan (played by Bruce Prochnik) who dares to ask for more food at the workhouse, is sent out into the cruel world, falls in with a band of juvenile pickpockets under the benign controlof Fagin (Clive Revill), and is eventually rescued from a life of fraternal crime by kindly, wealthy Mr. Brownlow (Geoffrey Lumb), who turns out to be Oliver's grandfather. Kenny's ingenious, atmospheric settings were much admired as were the tuneful, rousing score. The work, however, did not last long in a 1984 revival with Ron Moody (the London and 1968 film version Fagin) and Patti LuPone.

Five other Dickens novels were seen on Broadway in musical adaptations: *Barnaby Rudge (Dolly Varden,* 1902); *The Posthumous Papers of the Pickwick Club (Mr. Pickwick,* 1903; *Pickwick* 1965); *A Christmas Carol (Comin' Uptown,* 1979); *David Copperfield (Copperfield,* 1981); *The Mystery of Edwin Drood* 1985).

FUNNY GIRL

Music:
Jule Styne

Lyrics:
Bob Merrill

Book:
Isobel Lennart

Producer:
Ray Stark

Directors:
Jerome Robbins, Garson Kanin

Choreographer:
Carol Haney

Cast:
Barbra Streisand, Sydney Chaplin, Kay Medford, Danny Meehan, Jean Stapleton, Roger DeKoven, Joseph Macaulay, Lainie Kazan, Buzz Miller, George Reeder, Larry Fuller

Songs:
"I'm the Greatest Star"; "Cornet Man"; "I Want to Be Seen With You Tonight"; "People"; "You Are Woman"; "Don't Rain on My Parade"; "Sadie, Sadie"; "Who Are You Now?"; "The Music That Makes Me Dance"

New York run:
Winter Garden, March 26, 1964; 1,348 p.

Funny Girl. Barbra Streisand singing "I'm the Greatest Star" as Danny Meehan watches. (Henry Grossman)

The funny girl of the title refers to Fanny Brice, and the story, told mostly in flashback, covers the major events in the life of the celebrated comedienne — her discovery by impresario Florenz Ziegfeld, her triumphs in the *Ziegfeld Follies,* her infatuation with and stormy marriage to smooth-talking con man Nick Arnstein, and the breakup of that marriage after Nick has served time for masterminding the theft of Wall Street securities. Film producer Ray Stark, Miss Brice's son-in-law, had long wanted to make a movie based on the Fanny Brice story, but he became convinced that it should first be done on the stage. Mary Martin, Anne Bancroft, and Carol Burnett had all turned down the leading part before it was won by Barbra Streisand, whose only other Broadway experience had been in a supporting role in *I Can Get It for You Wholesale.* Miss Streisand succeeded so well — her recording of "People" was a hit before *Funny Girl* opened — that she became even more renowned than the woman she portrayed.

At first there was hope that the *Gypsy* team of Jule Styne and Stephen Sondheim would be reunited to write the score, but Sondheim wasn't interested and Styne contacted Bob Merrill. Some of their songs, however, virtually replaced those used in comparable situations in *Gypsy* — "I'm the Greatest Star" for "Some People," "Don't Rain on My Parade" for "Everything's Coming Up Roses," and "The Music That Makes Me Dance" (which suggested Fanny Brice's closely identified theme song, "My Man") for "Rose's Turn." When Jerome Robbins, the original director, walked out in a dispute with the author, he was succeeded by Bob Fosse, who didn't stay long, then by Garson Kanin, who quit after Robbins was lured back.

The musical was variously announced under such titles as *A Very Special Person, My Man,* and *The Luckiest People* before David Merrick (who was to have been the show's co-producer) suggested *Funny Girl.* Numerous script alterations — including 40 rewrites of the final scene alone — and five opening-night postponements were required before the show was considered ready for its official premiere. During the Broadway run, Miss Streisand was followed by Mimi Hines, and Sydney Chaplin, who played Nick Arnstein, by Johnny Desmond. The road company, which toured for 13 months was headed by Marilyn Michaels (Fanny), Anthony George (Nick), and Lillian Roth (Fanny's mother). Miss Streisand also starred in the 1968 film version and its 1975 sequel, *Funny Lady.*

Hello, Dolly!

Music & lyrics:
Jerry Herman

Book:
Michael Stewart

Producer:
David Merrick

Director-choreographer:
Gower Champion

Cast:
Carol Channing, David Burns, Eileen Brennan, Sondra Lee, Charles Nelson Reilly, Jerry Dodge, Gordon Connell, Igors Gavon, Alice Playten, David Hartman

Songs:
"It Takes a Woman"; "Put on Your Sunday Clothes"; "Ribbons Down My Back"; "Dancing"; "Before the Parade Passes By"; "Hello, Dolly!"; "It Only Takes a Moment"; "So Long, Dearie"

New York run:
St. James Theatre, January 16, 1964; 2,844 p.

For over ten months — until it was overtaken by *Fiddler on the Roof* — *Hello, Dolly!* held the record as Broadway's longest running musical. Its tryout tour, however, was hardly a harbinger of even a moderate success. New writers had to be called in, three songs were dropped and three added (including the first-act finale, "Before the Parade Passes By"), and Jerry Dodge replaced one of the two leading juveniles. But director Gower Champion made it all work and the musical won a rousing Broadway reception.

The turn-of-the-century tale centers around Dolly Gallagher Levi, a New York matchmaker engaged to help a pompous Yonkers merchant, Horace Vandergelder (David Burns), in his pursuit of a mate. But the matchmaker sets her cap for Vandergelder herself, and eventually he acknowledges that it fits. Along the way, the exuberant Dolly helps two of Vandergelder's clerks, Barnaby Tucker and Cornelius Hackl (Jerry Dodge and Charles Nelson Reilly) enjoy a night at the Harmonia Gardens restaurant with dressmaker Irene Malloy and her assistant Minnie Fay (Eileen Brennan and Sondra Lee). After her grand entrance into the restaurant, Dolly sets off a rousing, high-kicking reception by the waiters welcoming her back to a once favored haunt.

Hello, Dolly! had an unusually lengthy history. Its first version, in 1835, was a London play, *A Day Well Spent,* by John Oxenford. Seven years later, *Einen Jux Will er Sich Machen (He Wants to Have a Lark),* a Viennese variation by Johann Nestroy, was produced. In 1938, Thornton Wilder turned the Nestroy play into *The Merchant of Yonkers,* and 17 years after that he rewrote it as *The Matchmaker.* Both Wilder plays had Broadway runs. Another forerunner of *Hello, Dolly!* was the 1891 musical, *A Trip to Chinatown.*

Once Ethel Merman had turned down the chance to be the first song-and-dance Dolly, Carol Channing seized the opportunity to make it one of her two most closely identified roles. During the Broadway run she was succeeded by Ginger Rogers, Martha Raye, Betty Grable, Bibi Osterwald, Pearl Bailey (who starred in an all-black company and was frequently spelled by Thelma Carpenter), Phyllis Diller, and — at last — Ethel Merman. David Burns was replaced by Max Showalter, and Cab Calloway had the Vandergelder part opposite Miss Bailey. During Miss Merman's tenure, Russell Nype played Cornelius. The show returned to New York in 1974 with Miss Bailey and Billy Daniels leading an all-black cast, and in 1978 it came back with Miss Channing and Eddie Bracken as part of a year-and-a-half tour. In 1965, Mary Martin and Loring Smith headed the first touring company, which played the Far East (primarily for U.S. troops) and London. A second company toured two years nine months originally with Miss Channing (succeeded by Eve Arden and Dorothy Lamour) and Horace MacMahon. A third company, starring Miss Grable (then Miss Rogers and Miss Lamour) traveled for two years four months. The show's film version, released in 1969, co-starred Barbra Streisand and Walter Matthau.

FIDDLER ON THE ROOF

Music:
Jerry Bock

Lyrics:
Sheldon Harnick

Book:
Joseph Stein

Producer:
Harold Prince

Director-choreographer:
Jerome Robbins

Cast:
Zero Mostel, Maria Karnilova, Beatrice Arthur, Joanna Merlin, Austin Pendleton, Bert Convy, Julia Migenes, Michael Granger, Tanya Everett, Leonard Frey, Maurice Edwards

Songs:
"Tradition"; "Matchmaker, Matchmaker"; If I Were a Rich Man"; "Sabbath Prayer"; "To Life"; "Miracle of Miracles"; "Sunrise, Sunset"; "Now I Have Everything"; "Do You Love Me?"; "Far from the Home I Love"; "Anatevka"

New York run:
Imperial Theatre, September 22, 1964; 3,242 p.

Fiddler on the Roof. Tevye (Zero Mostel) is none too happy that daughter Tzeitel (Joanna Merlin) is marrying a poor tailor (Austin Pendleton). (Friedman-Abeles)

One of Broadway's classic musicals, *Fiddler on the Roof* defied the accepted rules of commercial success by dealing with persecution, poverty, and the problems of holding on to traditions in the midst of a hostile world. But despite a story and setting that many thought had limited appeal, the theme struck such a universal response that the fiddler was perched precariously on his roof for seven years nine months, thus becoming the longest running production — musical or non musical — in Broadway history. (The record, however, was broken by *Grease* in December 1979.)

The plot is set in the Jewish village of Anatevka, Russia, in 1905, and deals mainly with the efforts of Tevye (Zero Mostel), a dairyman, his wife Golde (Maria Karnilova), and their five daughters to cope with their harsh existence. Tzeitel (Joanna Merlin), the oldest daughter, marries a poor tailor (Austin Pendleton), after Tevye had promised her to a well-to-do middle-aged butcher (Michael Granger). Hodel (Julia Migenes), the second daughter, marries a revolutionary (Bert Convy) and follows him to Siberia. Chava (Tanya Everett), the third daughter, marries out of her religion. When, at the end, the Czar's Cossacks destroy Anatevka, Tevye, still holding on to his faith and his traditions, bravely prepares to take what's left of his family to America. Though Zero Mostel became closely identified with the role of Tevye he proved not to be indispensable, since the musical had no trouble continuing with his successors Luther Adler, Herschel Bernardi, Harry Goz, Jerry Jarrett, Paul Lipson, and Jan Peerce. Six actresses replaced Maria Karnilova as Golde, including Martha Schlamme, Dolores Wilson, and Peg Murray. During the Broadway engagement, Pia Zadora took over as Bielke, the youngest daughter, and Bette Midler was seen for a time as Tzeitel. In 1976, *Fiddler on the Roof* came back to New York with Mostel and Thelma Lee in the leading roles; in 1981, it returned — at Lincoln Center's New York State Theatre — with Herschel Bernardi and Maria Karnilova. The national tour, originally featuring Luther Adler and Dolores Wilson, was on the road for two years three months. Topol, who played Tevye in London, was seen in the 1971 screen version which also featured Norma Crane and Molly Picon.

The idea for *Fiddler on the Roof* was planted when Jerry Bock, Sheldon Harnick, and Joseph Stein decided to make a musical out of Sholom Aleichem's short story, "Tevye and His Daughters." They took the first draft to producer Harold Prince who advised them that no other director but Jerome Robbins could possibly give the material the universal quality that it required. The first choice for Tevye was Danny Kaye; among others considered at various times were Howard Da Silva, Tom Bosley, and Danny Thomas.

THE ROAR OF THE GREASEPAINT — THE SMELL OF THE CROWD

Music, lyrics & book:
Leslie Bricusse & Anthony Newley

Producer:
David Merrick

Director:
Anthony Newley

Choreographer:
Gillian Lynne

Cast:
Anthony Newley, Cyril Ritchard, Sally Smith, Gilbert Price, Joyce Jillson

Songs:
"A Wonderful Day Like Today"; "Where Would You Be Without Me?"; "My First Love Song"; "Look at That Face"; "The Joker"; "Who Can I Turn To?"; "Feeling Good"; "Nothing Can Stop Me Now!"; "My Way"; "Sweet Beginning"

New York run:
Shubert Theatre, May 16, 1965; 232 p.

The Roar of the Greasepaint — The Smell of the Crowd. Cyril Ritchard and Anthony Newley. (Henry Grossman)

The Roar of the Greasepaint — The Smell of the Crowd was another allegorical musical in the same style as the previous Anthony Newley-Leslie Bricusse *Stop the World — I Want to Get Off.* Again Newley starred and directed, Sean Kenny designed the symbolic set (this one resembling a huge gaming table), and David Merrick was the producer. Here the writers are concerned with the weighty theme of Playing the Game, which covers such universal topics as religion (the supplicating ballad, "Who Can I Turn To?," is addressed to God), hunger, work, love, success, death, and rebellion. Leading the cast were Cyril Ritchard as Sir, representing ruling class authority, and Anthony Newley as Cocky, representing the masses who submissively play the game according to the existing rules — no matter how unfair they are. In the end, emboldened by a character called The Negro (Gilbert Price), Cocky challenges Sir's dominance, and they both realize that power must be shared between them. Though the musical folded in England without opening in London, Merrick secured the American rights and sent the production on a 13½-week tryout tour, thus allowing the infectious music-hall type songs to win favor before the show reached Broadway.

Half a Sixpence

Music & lyrics:
David Heneker

Book:
Beverly Cross

Producers:
Allen-Hodgdon, Stevens Productions, Harold Fielding

Director:
Gene Saks

Choreographer:
Onna White

Cast:
Tommy Steel, Ann Shoemaker, James Grout, Carrie Nye, Polly James, Grover Dale, Will Mackenzie, John Cleese

Songs:
"Half a Sixpence"; "Money to Burn"; "She's Too Far Above Me"; "If the Rain's Got to Fall"; "Long Ago"; "Flash Bang Wallop"

New York run:
Broadhurst Theatre, April 25, 1965; 512 p.

Half a Sixpence. Tommy Steel playing the banjo for his pub cronies in the "Money to Burn" number. (Friedman-Abeles)

H.G. Wells' novel, *Kipps,* supplied the basis for this period musical in which Tommy Steele (for whom it was written) starred in London in 1963, in New York in 1965, and on film in 1967. *Half a Sixpence* is about Arthur Kipps, an orphan who becomes a draper's apprentice in Folkestone, England, at the turn of the century. Arthur inherits a fortune, becomes engaged to highborn Helen Walsingham (Carrie Nye), breaks off the engagement to marry Ann Pornick (Polly James), a working class girl, loses his money to Helen's brother (John Cleese) in a phony business scheme, and ends up contentedly as the owner of a book shop. There were some changes in the score for the New York engagement, which was enlivened by Onna White's rousing dances, especially the high kicking, banjo-plucking "Money to Burn." During the run, Steele was succeeded by Tony Tanner, Joel Grey, and Dick Kalman.

On a Clear Day You Can See Forever

Music:
Burton Lane

Lyrics & book:
Alan Jay Lerner

Producer:
Alan Jay Lerner

Director:
Robert Lewis

Choreographer:
Herbert Ross

Cast:
Barbara Harris, John Cullum, Titos Vandis, William Daniels, Clifford David, Rae Allen

Songs:
"Hurry! It's Lovely Up Here"; "On a Clear Day"; "On the S.S. Bernard Cohn"; "She Wasn't You"; "Melinda"; "What Did I Have That I Don't Have?"; "Wait Till We're Sixty-Five"; "Come Back to Me"

New York run:
Mark Hellinger Theatre, October 17, 1965; 280 p.

On a Clear Day You Can See Forever. John Cullum and Barbara Harris. (Bert Andrews)

Alan Jay Lerner's fascination with the phenomenon of extrasensory perception (ESP) led to his teaming with composer Richard Rodgers in 1962 to write a musical called *I Picked a Daisy*. When that partnership failed to work out, Lerner turned to Burton Lane, and the show was retitled *On a Clear Day You Can See Forever*. Though Barbara Harris was the only actress ever considered for the female lead, at least six actors were announced for the male lead until it went to Louis Jordan — and *he* was replaced by John Cullum during the Boston tryout. The musical (the first with a top ticket price of $11.90) is concerned with Daisy Gamble who can predict the future and, when hypnotized by Dr. Mark Bruckner, can also recall her life as Melinda Wells in 18th Century London. When Mark's infatuation with Melinda makes her something of a rival to the real-life alter ego, Daisy runs away. In the end, however, his stirring plea "Come Back to Me" is so persuasive that the couple is reunited. The 1970 film version starred Barbra Streisand and Yves Montand.

Do I Hear A Waltz?

Music:
Richard Rodgers

Lyrics:
Stephen Sondheim

Book:
Arthur Laurents

Producer:
Richard Rodgers

Director:
John Dexter

Choreographer:
Herbert Ross

Cast:
Elizabeth Allen, Sergio Franchi, Carol Bruce, Madeline Sherwood, Julienne Marie, Stuart Damon, Fleury D'Antonakis, Jack Manning

Songs:
"Someone Woke Up"; "This Week Americans"; "What Do We Do? We Fly!"; "Someone Like You"; "Here We Are Again"; "Take the Moment"; "Moon in My Window"; "We're Gonna Be All Right"; "Do I Hear a Waltz?"; "Stay"; "Thank You So Much"

New York run:
46th Street Theatre, March 18, 1965; 220 p.

Since Stephen Sondheim was something of a protégé of Oscar Hammerstein II it was almost inevitable that Richard Rodgers would team up with him after Hammerstein's death. Their single joint effort resulted in Do I Hear a Waltz?, which Arthur Laurents adapted from his own play, *The Time of the Cuckoo,* first produced in 1952. Taking place in Venice, the tale concerns Leona Samish (Elizabeth Allen), who has an intense but foredoomed affair with Renato Di Rossi (Sergio Franchi), a married shopkeeper. Though initially, there was to have been no dancing in the musical, the authors felt during the Boston tryout that the rueful story needed more movement and choreographer Herbert Ross was called in. His contribution was most apparent in the scene in which Leona — who has always been sure she will know true love if she hears an imaginary waltz — hears it, sings about it, and dances to it.

MAME

Music & lyrics:
Jerry Herman

Book:
Jerome Lawrence & Robert E. Lee

Producers:
Robert Fryer, Lawrence Carr, Sylvia & Joseph Harris

Director:
Gene Saks

Choreographer:
Onna White

Cast:
Angela Lansbury, Beatrice Arthur, Jane Connell, Willard Waterman, Frankie Michaels, Charles Braswell, Jerry Lanning

Songs:
"It's Today"; "Open a New Window"; "My Best Girl"; "We Need a Little Christmas"; "Mame"; "Bosom Buddies"; "That's How Young I Feel"; "If He Walked Into My Life"

New York run:
Winter Garden, May 24, 1966; 1,508 p.

Mame. Bosom buddies Angela Lansbury and Beatrice Arthur. (Friedman-Abeles)

Once Mary Martin had turned down the title role in Mame, some 40 other actresses had to be eliminated before the part went to Angela Lansbury — who quickly established herself as one of the reigning queens of Broadway. Her vehicle, the fifth longest running musical of the Sixties, was an adaptation of Patrick Dennis' novel, *Auntie Mame,* which had also been the basis of the 1954 play. The show's musical-comedy lineage, however, could be traced to *Hello, Dolly!,* since it again spotlighted an antic, middle-aged matchmaking widow, and it again had a bubbling score by Jerry Herman including another strutting title song.

Set mostly in and around Mame's home at 3 Beekman Place, New York, the tale covers the period from 1928 to 1946. Firmly dedicated to the credo that "Life is a banquet and most poor sons-of-bitches are starving to death," Mame Dennis brings up her orphaned nephew Patrick (Frankie Michaels) in an aggressively permissive atmosphere as she urges him to live life to the fullest by opening a new window every day. After being wiped out by the stock market crash, Mame lands a part in — and manages to ruin — a musical comedy starring her bosom buddy Vera Charles (Beatrice Arthur), then recoups her fortunes by marrying Southern aristocrat Beauregard Jackson Pickett Burnside (Charles Braswell). Even Beau's death climbing an Alp cannot deter the indomitable Mame, whose final triumph is steering Patrick out of the clutches of a birdbrained snob and into the arms of a more appropriate mate. During the Broadway run, Miss Lansbury was followed by Celeste Holm, Janis Paige, Jane Morgan, and Ann Miller. Heading the four road companies were, respectively, Miss Holm, Miss Lansbury, Susan Hayward, and Janet Blair. Miss Lansbury also starred in a 1983 Broadway revival which had a brief run. The 1974 Hollywood version found Miss Arthur repeating her original role in a cast headed by Lucille Ball and Robert Preston.

CABARET

Music:
John Kander

Lyrics:
Fred Ebb

Book:
Joe Masteroff

Producer-director:
Harold Prince

Choreographer:
Ron Field

Cast:
Jill Haworth, Jack Gilford, Bert Convy, Lotte Lenya, Joel Grey, Peg Murray, Edward Winter

Songs:
"Willkommen"; "Don't Tell Mama"; "Perfectly Marvelous"; "Two Ladies"; "It Couldn't Please Me More"; "Tomorrow Belongs to Me"; "The Money Song"; "Married"; "If You Could See Her"; "Cabaret"

New York run:
Broadhurst Theatre, November 20, 1966; 1,165 p.

Cabaret. Lotte Lenya and Jack Gilford singing "It Couldn't Please Me More." (Friedman-Abeles)

Claiming derivation from both Christopher Isherwood's *Berlin Stories* and John van Druten's 1951 dramatization, *I Am a Camera, Cabaret* turned a sleazy Berlin nightclub into a metaphor for the decadent world of pre-Hitler Germany, with the floorshow numbers used as commentaries on situations in the plot. At the Kit Kat Klub, where the epicene Master of Ceremonies (Joel Grey) bids one and all "Willkommen, bienvenue, welcome," the star attraction is the hedonistic British expatriate Sally Bowles (Jill Haworth), who also beckons customers with her own siren song to "Come to the cabaret, old chum." The main stories revolve around Sally's brief liaison with Clifford Bradshaw (Bert Convy), an American writer, and the more tragic romance between Fraulein Schneider (Lotte Lenya), a pragmatic landlady, and her Jewish suitor Herr Schultz (Jack Gilford). Helping to recreate the mood of a world in decay was the fluid direction of Harold Prince (it was his idea to add the Master of Ceremonies as a unifying symbol), a John Kander-Fred Ebb score that purposely evoked Kurt Weill, and the settings of Boris Aronson that recalled the paintings of George Grosz.

During the Broadway run, Miss Haworth was succeeded by Anita Gillette, Melissa Hart, and Tandy Cronyn. For the tour, which lasted one year seven months, the leads were taken by Miss Hart, Leo Fuchs (Schultz), Gene Rupert (Clifford), Signe Hasso (Fraulein), and Robert Salvio (MC). The 1972 film version retained Joel Grey (who also starred in the 1987 Broadway revival), but added Liza Minnelli, Michael York, Marisa Berenson, and a new story line.

Cabaret. "Willkommen, bienvenue, welcome," sings Joel Grey. (Friedman-Abeles)

I Do! I Do!

Music:
Harvey Schmidt

Lyrics & book:
Tom Jones

Producer:
David Merrick

Director:
Gower Champion

Cast:
Mary Martin, Robert Preston

Songs:
"I Love My Wife";
"My Cup Runneth Over";
"Love Isn't Everything";
"Nobody's Perfect";
"The Honeymoon Is Over";
"Where Are the Snows?";
"When the Kids Get Married";
"Someone Needs Me";
"Roll Up the Ribbons"

New York run:
46th Street Theatre, December 5, 1966; 560 p.

I Do! I Do! Robert Preston and Mary Martin. (Friedman-Abeles)

I Do! I Do! may have been the first Broadway musical ever to have a cast consisting entirely of two people, but since those people were Mary Martin and Robert Preston, no one could possibly have felt the need for anyone else on stage. In all other ways, however, the musical — which was adapted from Jan de Hartog's 1951 play, *The Fourposter* — was an ambitious undertaking, covering 50 years in the life of a married couple, Agnes and Michael, from their wedding day to the day they move out of their house. In between, they bring up a family, quarrel, threaten to break up, have a reconciliation, plan for a life without children in the house, and reveal in song exactly what they mean to each other. Apart from its stars, who were followed on Broadway by Carol Lawrence and Gordon MacRae, the production was especially noted for Gower Champion's inventive direction. A later musical with only two characters — but each with three alter egos — was the 1979 hit, *They're Playing Our Song.*

Zorba

Music:
John Kander

Lyrics:
Fred Ebb

Book:
Joseph Stein

Producer-director:
Harold Prince

Choreographer:
Ron Field

Cast:
Herschel Bernardi, Maria Karnilova, John Cunningham, Carmen Alvarez, Lorraine Serabian, James Luisi

Songs:
"Life Is"; "The First Time"; "The Top of the Hill"; "No Boom Boom"; "The Butterfly"; "Only Love"; "Y'assou"; "Happy Birthday"; "I Am Free"

New York run:
Imperial Theatre, November 17, 1968; 305 p.

Zorba. Maria Karnilova and Herschel Bernardi in the "Y'assou" number. (Friedman-Abeles)

Although it reunited the *Cabaret* team of composer John Kander, lyricist Fred Ebb, and producer-director Harold Prince, *Zorba* was more of an Aegean counterpart to *Fiddler on the Roof,* with its larger-than-life aging hero and its stageful of earthy, ethnic types. It also had the same producer, librettist, set designer (Boris Aronson), and costume designer (Patricia Zipprodt), and its leading roles were played by two *Fiddler* alumni, Herschel Bernardi and Maria Karnilova. The story, however, was far grimmer, and the people of Crete a colder, more menacing lot than the colorful villagers of Anatevka. The tale involves the ebulient Zorba (Bernardi) with a studious young man named Nikos (John Cunningham) who has inherited an abandoned mine on the island of Crete. This sets off a series of tragic events, including the suicide of a Cretan youth out of unrequited love for a young Widow (Carmen Alvarez), the vengeful murder of the Widow by the youth's family, the discovery that the mine is inoperable, and the death of Hortense (Maria Karnilova), a coquettish French cocotte in love with Zorba. Nothing, however, can dampen Zorba's lust for life and his determination to live it to the fullest.

The production, the first to charge $15 for Saturday night orchestra seats, was based on Nikos Kazantzakis's novel *Zorba the Greek,* which became a 1964 movie with Anthony Quinn and Lila Kedrova, directed by Michael Cacoyannis. Cacoyannis also directed Quinn and Kedrova in a new production of the musical in 1983. It began its cross-country tour early in the year, had a longer Broadway run than the original, then toured again through July 1986.

THE HAPPY TIME

Music:
John Kander

Lyrics:
Fred Ebb

Book:
N. Richard Nash

Producer:
David Merrick

Director-choreographer:
Gower Champion

Cast:
Robert Goulet, David Wayne, Mike Rupert, Julie Gregg, George S. Irving, Charles Durning

Songs:
"The Happy Time"; "Tomorrow Morning"; "Please Stay"; "I Don't Remember You"; "The Life of the Party"; "Seeing Things"; "A Certain Girl"

New York run:
Broadway Theatre, January 18, 1968; 286 p.

A gentle, nostalgic look at a French-Canadian family, *The Happy Time* was adapted from the novel by Robert Fontaine and the play by Samuel Taylor. The story is primarily concerned with the coming of age of Bibi Bonnard (Mike Rupert) and his desire to see the world with his Uncle Jacques (Robert Goulet), a footloose magazine photographer who has returned to his family for a brief visit. But Bibi's plans to run off with Jacques are opposed by the usually permissive Grandpère Bonnard (David Wayne) who manages — with Jacques' help — to convince Bibi to remain at home. The use of blow-up photographs to establish the mood for the various scenes was one of director Gower Champion's most effective touches. *The Happy Time* bore a certain resemblance to *110 in the Shade,* a previous musical by N. Richard Nash that had also been presented by David Merrick. That one also offered a smooth-talking visitor to a small town who excites the people's imagination, and leaves them with renewed appreciation of their own values.

COMPANY

Music & lyrics:
Stephen Sondheim

Book:
George Furth

Producer-director:
Harold Prince

Choreographer:
Michael Bennett

Cast:
Dean Jones, Elaine Stritch, Barbara Barrie, John Cunningham, Charles Kimbrough, Donna McKechnie, Charles Braswell, Susan Browning, Steve Elmore, Beth Howland, Pamela Myers, Merle Louise

Songs:
"Company"; "The Little Things You Do Together"; "Sorry-Grateful"; "You Could Drive a Person Crazy"; "Someone Is Waiting"; "Another Hundred People"; "Getting Married Today"; "What Would We Do Without You?"; "Barcelona"; "The Ladies who Lunch"; "Being Alive"

New York run:
Alvin Theatre, April 26, 1970; 706 p.

Company. Susan Browning, Donna McKechnie, and Pamela Myers. (Martha Swope)

Company was the first of six Broadway musicals created by the most influential and daring team of the Seventies, composer-lyricist Stephen Sondheim and director Harold Prince. In putting this work together they avoided the conventional dramatic structure of the linear story by using five separate stories dealing with marriage that were held together by a single character who influences and is influenced by his "good and crazy" married friends. Moreover, it was a bold example of the concept musical — in which the style of telling is as important as what is being told — with songs used as commentaries on the situations and characters, and the actors performing in a cage-like skeletal setting (by Boris Aronson) that made use of stairways, an elevator, and projections.

Initially, *Company* was a collection of 11 one-act plays by George Furth. Prince, however, saw it as a musical reflecting how life in a big city influences various couples, and Furth then revised three of the plays and added two others. The character of the bachelor Robert was brought in to connect the episodes, with the occasion of his 35th birthday party used as a framework. While the couples are less than idyllically happy — they fight, make plans to divorce, smoke pot, drink too much — the general philosophy, summed up in Robert's closing solo "Being Alive," is that it's better to be married than single.

Because of illness, Dean Jones, the original Robert, was replaced by Larry Kert within a month after the Broadway opening. During the run, Elaine Stritch, as a middle-aged guzzler who has the sardonic show-stopper "The Ladies who Lunch," was succeeded by Jane Russell and Vivian Blaine. The show's yearlong tour had a cast headed by George Chakiris and Miss Stritch.

FOLLIES

Music & lyrics:
Stephen Sondheim

Book:
James Goldman

Producer:
Harold Prince

Directors:
Harold Prince & Michael Bennett

Choreographer:
Michael Bennett

Cast:
Alexis Smith, Gene Nelson, Dorothy Collins, John McMartin, Yvonne DeCarlo, Fifi D'Orsay, Mary McCarty, Ethel Shutta, Arnold Moss, Ethel Barrymore Colt, Michael Bartlett, Sheila Smith, Justine Johnston, Virginia Sandifur, Kurt Peterson, Victoria Mallory, Marti Rolph

Songs:
"Waiting for the Girls Upstairs"; "Ah, Paris!"; "Broadway Baby"; "The Road You Didn't Take"; "In Buddy's Eyes"; "Who's That Woman?"; "I'm Still Here"; "Too Many Mornings"; "The Right Girl"; "Could I Leave You?"; "Losing My Mind"; "The Story of Lucy and Jessie"

New York run:
Winter Garden, April 4, 1971; 522 p.

Follies. Alexis Smith singing "Could I Leave You?" (Martha Swope)

Taking place at a reunion of performers who had appeared in various editions of the *Weismann Follies* (a fictitious counterpart of the Ziegfeld revue), the musical dealt with the reality of life as contrasted with the unreality of the theatre, a theme it explored principally through the lives of two couples, the upper-class, unhappy Phyllis and Ben Stone (Alexis Smith and John McMartin) and the middle-class, unhappy Sally and Buddy Plummer (Dorothy Collins and Gene Nelson). The second of the Stephen Sondheim-Harold Prince musicals, *Follies* also depicted these couples as they were in their youth, a flashback device that prompted the composer to come up with songs purposely reminiscent of the styles of some of the theatre's great songwriters of the past. In 1985, a highly acclaimed all-star concert version was staged at Avery Fisher Hall. The musical bore a certain kinship with *Company,* which also was about jaded, ambivalent characters, took a disenchanted view of marriage, and used the structural device of a party to bring a group of people together.

JESUS CHRIST SUPERSTAR

Music: **Andrew Lloyd Webber**

Lyrics: **Tim Rice**

Conception: **Tom O'Horgan**

Producer: **Robert Stigwood**

Director: **Tom O'Horgan**

Cast:
Jeff Fenholt, Yvonne Elliman, Ben Vereen, Barry Dennen, Anita Morris

Songs:
"Heaven on Their Minds"; "What's the Buzz?"; "Everything's Alright"; "I Don't Know How to Love Him"; "King Herod's Song"; "Could We Start Again, Please?"; "Superstar"

New York run:
Mark Hellinger Theatre, October 12, 1971; 720 p.

Even though conceived as a theatre work, *Jesus Christ Superstar* appeared as a record before being presented on the stage because composer Andrew Lloyd Webber and lyricist Tim Rice were unable to find a producer willing to take a chance on so daring a production. Once it became a Gold Record album, however, the path was smoothed for its Broadway premiere. The self-described "rock opera" retold the last seven days of Christ in such a flamboyant, campy, and mind-blowing fashion that despite a mixed press and the opposition from various religious groups the show became a media hype and a boxoffice hit. The movie version was released in 1973 with Ted Neeley and Carl Anderson.

GODSPELL

Music & lyrics:
Stephen Schwartz

Book:
John-Michael Tebelak

Producers:
Edgar Lansbury, Stuart Duncan, Jospeh Beruh

Director:
John-Michael Tebelak

Cast:
Lamar Alford, David Haskell, Johanne Jonas, Robin Lamont, Sonia Manzano, Jeffrey Mylett, Stephen Nathan

Songs:
"Prepare Ye the Way of the Lord"; "Save the People"; "Day by Day"; "All for the Best"; "All Good Gifts"; "Light of the World"; "Turn Back, O Man"; "We Beseech Thee"; "On the Willows"

New York run:
Cherry Lane Theatre, May 17, 1971; 2,651 p.

The Seventies brought the Bible to the New York musical stage. Genesis supplied the source of both *Two by Two* (Noah and the Ark) in 1970 and *Joseph and the Amazing Technicolor Dreamcoat* in 1976 (performed at the Brooklyn Academy of Music); the Gospel According to St. Matthew was the origin of *Godspell* in 1971, *Jesus Christ Superstar* also in 1971, and *Your Arms Too Short to Box With God* in 1976. *Godspell* was a whimsical retelling of the last seven days of Christ, with Jesus in clownlike makeup sporting a superman "S" on his shirt; his disciples dressed like flower children; and the parables enacted in a frolicsome, contemporary manner. The work was first shown in nonmusical form as a workshop production at Café La Mama. When it was decided to turn *Godspell* into a musical, songs were then added by Stephen Schwartz. The show was presented in a Greenwich Village theatre for three months, then moved to the Promenade (on Broadway and 76th Street) for a total run of 2,124 performances, making it currently the fourth longest running Off-Broadway musical. The show's official "on" Broadway opening took place June 22, 1976, at the Broadhurst, where it ran for 527 performances. At one time there were seven road companies touring the United States. Godspell was revived in 1988 and gave 248 Off-Broadway performances. The film version, released in 1973, featured Victor Garber and David Haskell.

TWO GENTLEMEN OF VERONA

Music:
Galt MacDermot

Lyrics:
John Guare

Book:
John Guare & Mel Shapiro

Producer:
Joseph Papp for the New York Shakespeare Festival

Director:
Mel Shapiro

Choreographer:
Jean Erdman

Cast:
Jonelle Allen, Diana Davila, Clifton Davis, Raul Julia, Norman Matlock, Alix Elias, John Bottoms, Stockard Channing

Songs:
"Follow the Rainbow"; "Bring All the Boys Back Home"; "Night Letter"; "Who Is Silvia?" (lyric: Shakespeare); "Calla Lily Lady"

New York run:
St. James Theatre, December 1, 1971; 627 p.

Two Gentlemen of Verona was originally scheduled to be presented without songs as part of the New York Shakespeare Festival's series of free productions in Central Park. At the recommendation of director Mel Shapiro, a rock score was added to help give the modern adaptation of the play the proper contemporary flavor. The show proved so popular in its open-air presentation in the Summer of 1971 that it was transferred to Broadway, where its blend of anachronistic colloquialisms, ethnic references, and the Bard's own words (the song "Who Is Silvia?" uses the original text) won a receptive audience. The story spins the tale of two Veronese friends, the noble Valentine (Clifton Davis) and the ignoble Proteus (Raul Julia), whose adventures in Milan are complicated by Julia (Diana Davila), who loves Proteus, and Silvia (Jonelle Allen), who Loves Valentine.

CAMELOT
(From "CAMELOT")

Words by ALAN JAY LERNER
Music by FREDERICK LOEWE

Cdim C7

lim - it to the snow here ___ In

F F6 Fmaj7 F6 F F6

Cam - e - lot.

Fmaj7 F6 F Fmaj7 Bb Gb F

The win - ter is for - bid - den till De -

mf

Fmaj7

cem - ber ___ And ex - its March the

Bb
Gb
F
Cdim
sec - ond on the dot.
By
C7
Cdim
C7
or - der sum - mer lin - gers through Sep - tem - ber
E7
A
in Cam - e - lot.
mp
A7
D
Dmaj7
Cam - e - lot!
Cam - e - lot!

D6
D
Dmaj7
D6
D
Em
Cam - e - lot!
Cam - e - lot!
I know it
I know it
Dmaj7
Em
D
Em
Dmaj7
Em
sounds a bit bi - zarre,
gives a per - son pause,
D
F
But in Cam - e - lot,
But in Cam - e - lot,
mf
Cdim
Gm7
Dm6
Cam - e - lot,
Cam - e - lot,
That's how con - di - tions
Those are the le - gal

C9 Cdim Gm7 Dm6 C C7
are. The
laws. The
mp
F F6 Fmaj7 F6 F
rain may nev - er fall till af - ter sun - down. By
snow may nev - er slush up - on the hill - side. By
Fmaj7 B♭ G♭ F Cdim
eight the morn - ing fog must dis - ap - pear. In
nine P. M. the moon - light must ap - pear. In
C7 F A7 Dm7 F7
short, there's sim - ply not a more con - gen - ial spot For
short, there's sim - ply not a more con - gen - ial spot For

Bb Cdim Gm Bbm F Bb F Bb F Bb F
hap - p'ly - ev - er - af - ter - ing than here in
hap - p'ly - ev - er - af - ter - ing than here in
poco rit.
a tempo
C7sus C7 F
Cam - e - lot!
Cam - e -
accel.
C7sus C9 Bb A Am C7 F C7 F6 C
The lot!
mf
Bb Cdim C7 C7sus F
rall. e dim.

IF EVER I WOULD LEAVE YOU

(From "CAMELOT")

Words by Alan Jay Lerner
Music by Frederick Loewe

Cm7 F7 F9 Bbmaj9 Bb6
Tacet
shame! But if I'd ev - er leave you, It could-n't be in au - tumn.
Bbmaj9 Bdim F7 Gdim F7 Bbdim F7-9 Bbmaj9 Bb6 Dm Bb7
How I'd leave in au - tumn I nev - er will know. I've seen how you
Eb Cm F7 Bbmaj9 Bbmaj7 Cm7 G7
Tacet
spar - kle When fall nips the air. I know you in au - tumn
Cm Cm7 F7-9 Bb Ebm Bb D D+ D6 G A7
And I must be there. And could I leave you run - ning mer-ri - ly through the
R.H.
D Dmaj7 D6 F# B F# Em7 A7
snow? Or on a win - try eve - ning when you catch the fi - re's

D F7 F9
glow? If Ev - er I Would Leave You, How could it be in
Bbmaj9 Fdim Cm7 F Gdim F7
spring - time, Know - ing how in spring I'm be - witched by you
D7sus D7 Gm7 Dm Bb7 Eb Ebmaj7 Cm7 Ebm
so? Oh, no! not in spring - time! Sum - mer, win - ter or
f
mf
Bb C9 F9 Cm7 F7-9
fall! No, nev - er could I leave you at
pp subito
1 Bb6
all! And could I
mp
2 Bb6 B6 Bb
all!
cresc.
f
8va

MAKE SOMEONE HAPPY
(From "DO RE MI")

Words by BETTY COMDEN & ADOLPH GREEN
Music by JULE STYNE

Abm6
Bb7-9
Eb
One face that lights when it nears you, One {man / girl} you're
Gm7
Fm7
Bb7-9
Eb
Eb+
ev' - ry - thing to. Fame,
Eb6
Eb
Eb+
Eb6
Bbm7
if you win it, Comes and goes in a min - ute. Where's the real
Eb7
Ab
Ab+
stuff in life to cling to? Love
mf

Ab6
Abm6
Bb7-9
is the an - swer, Some - one to love is the an - swer.
Eb
Eb6
Ebmaj7
Cm7
Gm7
C9
Once you've found {him, her,} Build your world a - round {him, her,}
Fm7
Bb7
Eb
Gm7
C7-9
Make some - one hap - py, Make just one some - one hap - py
f
Fm7
Bb7-5
Fm7
Bb7
Eb
And you will be hap - py too.
mf
rall. e dim.
p

Soon It's Gonna Rain

Words by TOM JONES
Music by HARVEY SCHMIDT

Moderately

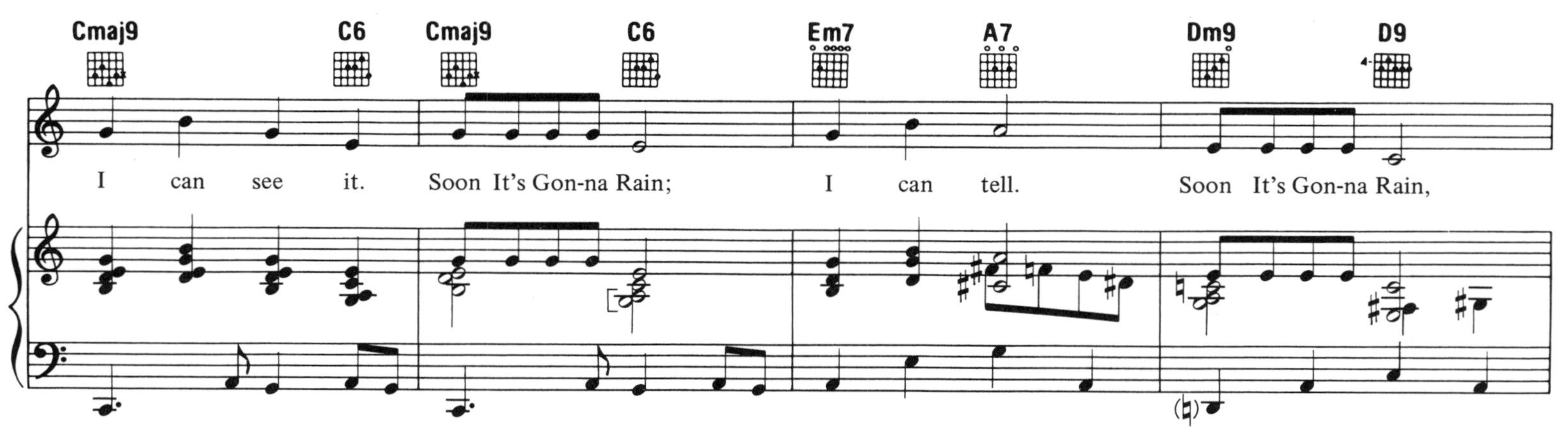

Cmaj9 C6 Cmaj9 C6 Em7 A7
I can feel it. Soon It's Gon-na Rain, I can tell.
Dm7 D9 Dm7 G7-9 C6
Soon It's Gon-na Rain; What-'ll we do with you?
We'll
Dm7 Em7 F6 G7 Cmaj9 C6 Em7 Am7
find four limbs of a tree. We'll build four walls and a floor. We'll
mf
Dm7 Fmaj7 Am7 D9 Dm7 G7
bind it o-ver with leaves, Then duck in-side to stay.
3

Cmaj9
C6
Cmaj9
C6
Cmaj9
C6
Em7
A7
Then we'll let it rain. We'll not feel it. Then we'll let it rain, Rain pell mell.
mf
Dm9
D9
Dm7
G7-9
Em7
A9
And we'll not com-plain If it nev-er stops at all We'll
Dm7
Em7
F6
G7sus
G7-9
C9
live and love with-in our own four walls.
mp
1
G7
2
pp

TRY TO REMEMBER
(From "THE FANTASTICKS")

Em7 Am7 D7 Gmaj7 Cmaj7 F
mem - ber the kind of Sep - tem - ber when you were a ten - der and cal - low
mem - ber when life was so ten - der that love was an em - ber a - bout to
cem - ber, it's nice to re - mem - ber the fire of Sep - tem - ber that made us
dim. rit.
D7 G Am D7
fel - low. Try to re - mem - ber and if you re - mem - ber then
bil - low. Try to re - mem - ber and if you re - mem - ber then
mel - low. Deep in De - cem - ber our hearts should re - mem - ber and
mp a tempo
1,2 G Cmaj7 D7
fol - low. (Echo) Fol - low, fol - low, fol - low, fol - low, fol - low, fol - low, fol - low, fol - low,
3 G
fol - low.
Cmaj7 D7 G
(Echo) Fol - low, fol - low, fol - low, fol - low, fol - low, fol - low, fol - low, fol - low, fol - low.
dim. pp

NEVER WILL I MARRY

By FRANK LOESSER

fan - cy danc - y fid - dle and free. Any flim - sy dim - sy
fp
look - ing for true love bet - ter waste no time, no time on
fp
Rhythmically
me.
Refrain
E♭
Nev - er, nev - er
f
p
Dm
will I mar - ry,
E♭
nev - er nev - er

Dm
Gm
A♭
will I wed.
Born to wan - der
D
E♭
Dsus
D
sol - i - tar - y. __
Wide my world,
A7
D
B♭
E♭
nar - row my bed.
Nev - er, nev - er, nev - er __
Dm
E♭
Cm9
will I mar - ry,
born to wan - der

Cm7/F
B♭
E♭
'til I'm dead.
No bur-dens
cresc.
f
Dm
to bear,
no con-science
nor care.
E♭
Dm
Gm
No mem-'ries
to mourn,
no turn - ing,
for I was
A♭
D
E♭
born to wan - der sol - i - tar - y,
p

Dsus
D
A7
D
B♭
Wide my world, nar - row my bed. Nev - er,
E♭
Dm
nev - er, nev - er ___ will I mar - ry.
cresc.
E♭
Cm9
Cm7/F
Born to wan - der 'til I'm
f
B♭
dead. ___
ff
pp

Our Language Of Love

Music by MARGUERITE MONNOT
Orig. French words by ALEXANDRE BREFFORT
English words by JULIAN MORE,
DAVID HENEKER, MONTY NORMAN

Eb6 F7 Bb7 Eb
-stand That the si- lence is bro- ken By our lan- guage of love.
Eb Ab Ab6 Abmaj7
It's clear to you, It's clear to me This pre-cious mo- ment had to
mf
Ab6 Gm C7 Fm
be Oth- er mo- ments out- class- ing Guard-ian an- gels are pass-
mp mf p
Bb7 Eb Eb6 Ebmaj7
ing No words will do, No lips can say The ten-der mean- ing we con-
mp
Eb6 F7 Bb7 Eb
vey, "I love you" is un- spo- ken, In our lan- guage of love.
rit.

I AIN'T DOWN YET
(From "THE UNSINKABLE MOLLY BROWN")

Words and Music by MEREDITH WILLSON

Bb Edim Bb7/F Eb F#dim Bb7/F Edim
me. You'll see me car - ried shoul - der high,
Bb7/F Bb7 Bb7+5 Eb Eb7
By fa - mous peo - ple I've nev - er met, But till I leave the rear,
Ab B7 Eb/Bb Bb7 Eb
it's from the rear you'll hear, "I Ain't Down Yet."
Edim Bb7/F Edim Bb7/F Edim Bb7/F Edim
Tacet
To show that you know, you got to show you know you
Bb7/F Bb7 Eb B7 Eb
know! I'm goan' to Yet."
sfz

I BELIEVE IN YOU

(From "HOW TO SUCCEED IN BUSINESS WITHOUT REALLY TRYING")

Words and Music by FRANK LOESSER

G D G Cmaj7 Db7 D7 G
You, I Be - lieve In You.
R.H.
G#dim G Eb7 Ab Bbm7 Eb7-5 Ab
I hear the And when my faith in my fel - low man
Bbm7 Db9 Cm7 F7 Bb Cm7 F7
all but falls a - part, I've but to feel your hand
Bb Gm7 C7 D7sus D7 G#dim
grasp - ing mine and I take heart, I take heart. To see the
rit.

Am7
D9
C
C#m7
F#7
Bm
C
cool clear eyes of a seek-er of wis-dom and truth,
Bm
G#dim
Am7
D9
C
C#m7
F#7
Yet there's that slam bang tang rem - i - nis-cent of gin and ver -
B
C
B
Cmaj7
Db7
D7
G
mouth. Oh I Be - lieve In You,
Cmaj7
Db7
D7
Cmaj7
D11
Gmaj7
I Be - lieve In You.
R.H.

Brotherhood Of Man

Handclapping Spiritual Feel

By FRANK LOESSER

C
C9
F
F#dim
B7
tie that binds
all hu - man hearts and minds
in - to one
proud to be
in that fra - ter - ni - ty,
the great big
mp
f
mf
1
C
F/C
C
D7
G7
Dm7
G7
Broth - er - hood Of Man.
Your life - long
mp
mf
2
C
Am
Dm7
G7
C
G7
Broth - er - hood Of Man?
mp
mf
f
C
G7
C
Cmaj7
Man?

MILK AND HONEY
(From "MILK AND HONEY")

Words and Music by
JERRY HERMAN

Dm7 E7 Am D7 Fm6 G7
hopes of the home-less and the dreams of the lost com - bine.
plans for to-mor-row some how e - ven to-day looks fine so
C Cmaj7 F E7 Am F#dim7 C Dm7 G7
This is the land that heav - en blessed and this love-ly land is
what if it's rock and dust and sand, for this love-ly land is
1 C Am C Am
mine.
2 C Am C Dm7 G7 C Am
mine. This love-ly land is mine.
Repeat ad lib and Fade

THE SWEETEST SOUNDS
(From "NO STRINGS")

Words and Music by
RICHARD RODGERS

E7
A7
Dm
hear Are still in- side my head.
Gm
The kind- est words I'll ev- er
Gm7
C7
Fmaj7
F6
know Are wait- ing to be said.
Gm6
A7
Dm
Gm
The most en- tranc- ing sight of
E7
A7
Cm7
all is yet for me to see.

F7
Bb
G7
Bdim
F6
And the dear- est love in all the
F
Gm7
C7
Fmaj7
world Is wait- ing some- where for me.
F7
Bb6
Gm7
C7
Is wait- ing some- where, Some- where for
1.
F
Fmaj7
Gm
A7
me.
The
mf
mp
2.
F
Gb6
F6
me.
mf
f
sf

I've Got Your Number

Lyric by CAROLYN LEIGH
Music by CY COLEMAN

E9 E7-9 Amaj7 D9 Bbm7 Eb9
But you're un - sure a lot,__ You're a lot__ like me. Oh,
G6 Dm7 G6 Dm7 G6 Dm7 G6 Gdim G7
I've Got Your Num - ber__ And what you're look - ing__ for
C6 Gm7 C6 Cdim C7 C6 Gm7 C7
And what you're look - ing__ for just suits me fine!
Ab7 Dbmaj9 Ab6 Bbm7 Bdim Cm7 Ab9
We'll break the rules a lot,__ We'll be damn'__ fools a lot,__

Dbmaj7
Ab6
Fm7
Bb9
Ab9
But then why should we not, How could we not com - bine, when
G6
Dm7
G7
I've Got Your Num - ber and I've got the glow you've got, I've Got Your
Num - ber and ba - by, You know you've got mine!
1
C6
Cmaj7
2
F
Dbmaj9
mine!

Real Live Girl

Lyric by CAROLYN LEIGH
Music by CY COLEMAN

D9
G6
E7
A7
arm- ful of Real Live Girl.
hunk of a Real Live Girl.
D9
G7
Par- don me if your af-
Speak- ing of mir- a- cles.
f
G7+5
Cmaj7
-fec- tion- ate squeeze Fogs up my
this must be it. Just when I
F7(+11)
gog- gles and buck- les my knees.
start- ed to learn how to knit.
G
E9
Am7
I'm sim- ply drowned in the sight and the
I'm all in stitch- es from find- ing what
mf

D7
B7+5
B7
sound and the scent and the
rich- es a waltz can re-
E7+5
E7
Em7
feel of a Real
veal with a
A9
Am7
D7
1. G
Live
Girl.
Em7
Am7
D7
2. G
Am7
C
G
Girl.
rit.

GONNA BUILD A MOUNTAIN

(From the Musical Production "STOP THE WORLD — I WANT TO GET OFF")

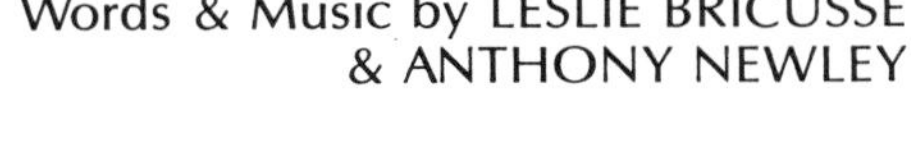

Words & Music by LESLIE BRICUSSE
& ANTHONY NEWLEY

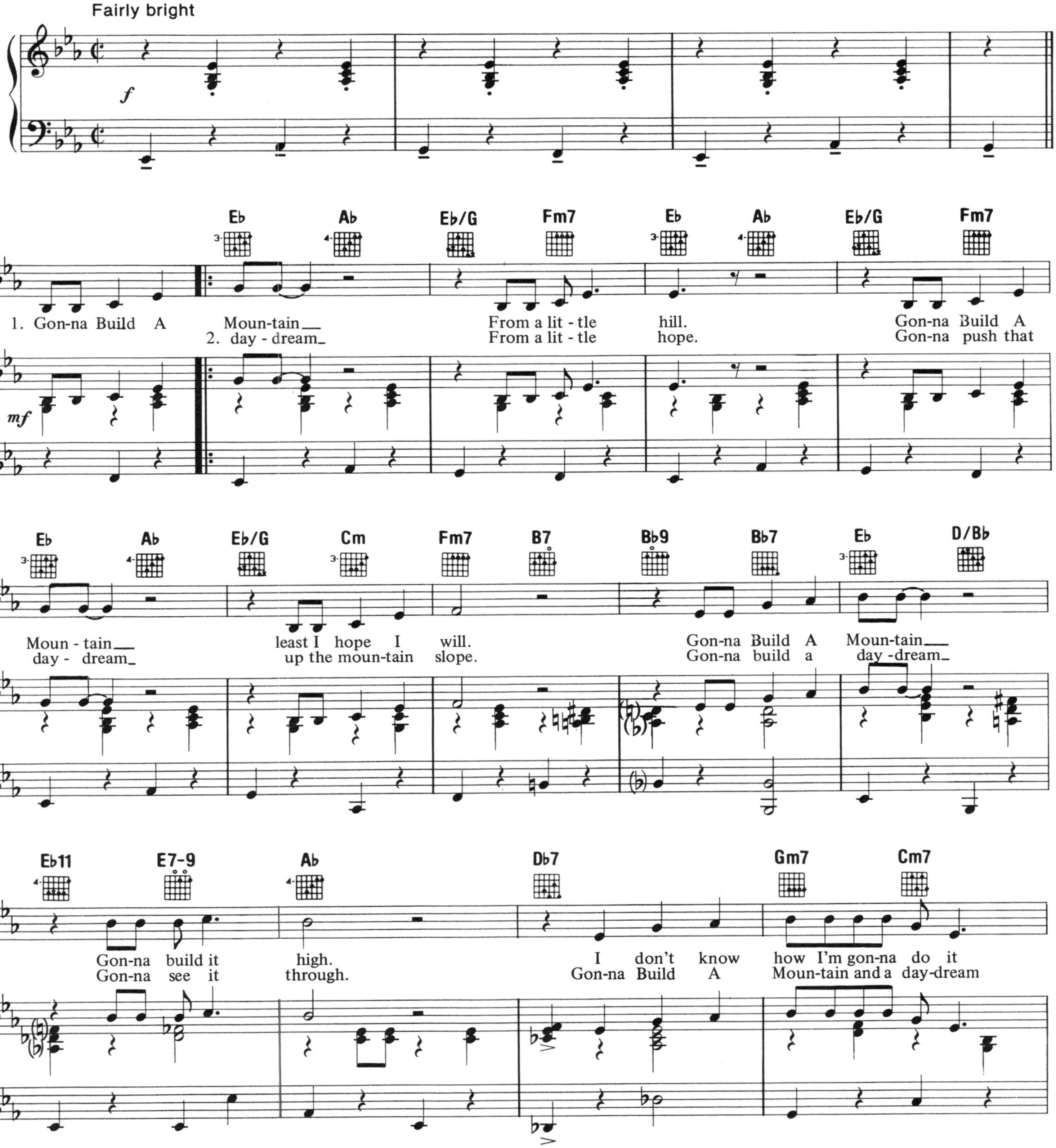
Fairly bright
f
Eb Ab Eb/G Fm7 Eb Ab Eb/G Fm7
1. Gon-na Build A Moun-tain From a lit-tle hill. Gon-na Build A
2. day-dream From a lit-tle hope. Gon-na push that
mf
Eb Ab Eb/G Cm Fm7 B7 Bb9 Bb7 Eb D/Bb
Moun-tain least I hope I will. Gon-na Build A Moun-tain
day-dream up the moun-tain slope. Gon-na build a day-dream
Eb11 E7-9 Ab Db7 Gm7 Cm7
Gon-na build it high. I don't know how I'm gon-na do it
Gon-na see it through. Gon-na Build A Moun-tain and a day-dream

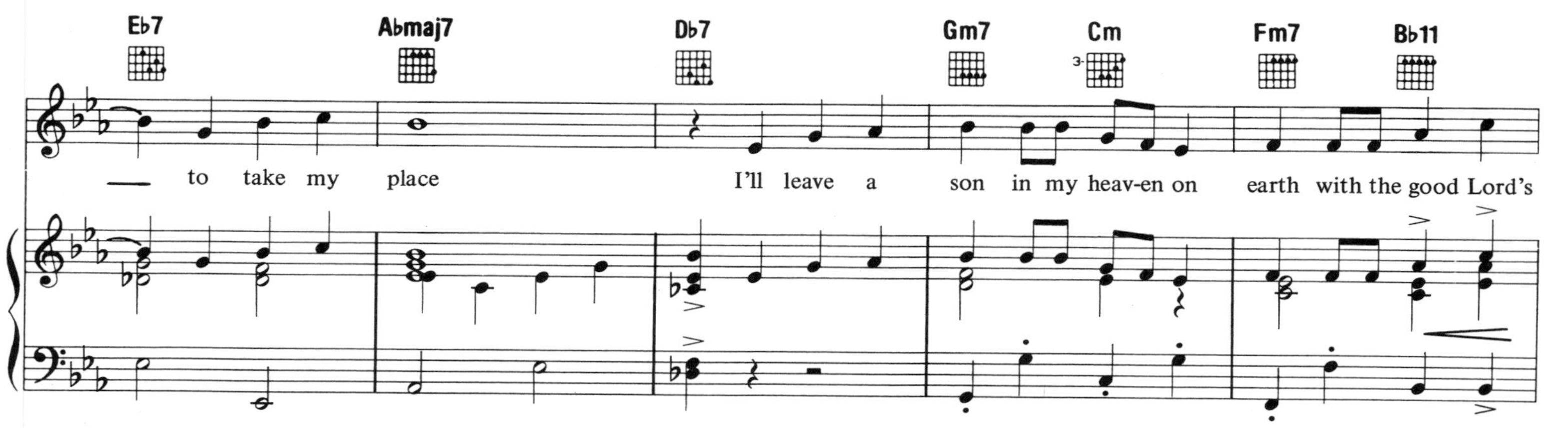

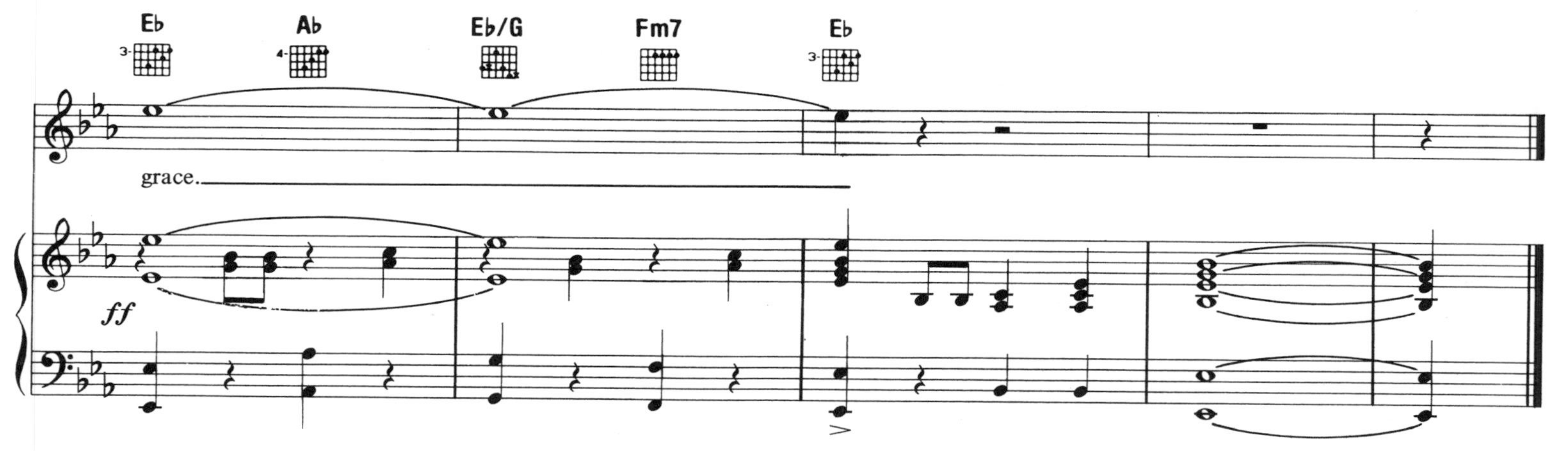

Verse 3. Gon-na build a heaven from a little hell.
Gon-na build a heaven and I know darn well.
If I build my mountain with a lot of care.
And take my daydream up the mountain heaven will be waiting there.

Verse 4. When I've built that heaven as I will some day
And the Lord sends Gabriel to take me away,
Wanna fine young son to take my place
I'll leave a son in my heav-en on earth,
With the Lord's good grace.

ONCE IN A LIFETIME

(From the Musical Production "STOP THE WORLD - I WANT TO GET OFF")

Words and Music by LESLIE BRICUSSE and ANTHONY NEWLEY

Fm7
E♭maj7
E♭7
A♭maj7
Gm7♭5
C7♭9
my once in a life - time, when
Fm7
Gm7
Fm7
Gm
Cm7
F7sus
F7
Fm7
B♭7
E7♭5
I can ex-plore a new and ex - cit - ing land. For
E♭
B♭m7/E♭
once in my life - time I feel like a gi - ant,
E♭
A♭
I soar like an ea - gle as tho' I had

B♭m E♭7 B♭m7 E♭7 A♭maj7 Gm7 Fm7 E♭maj7 E♭7
wings. For this is my mo - ment, my
A♭maj7 Gm7♭5 C7♭9 Fm7 Gm7
des - ti - ny calls me, and tho' it may be just
Fm7 Dm7/G G7 Cm7 F7♭5 Fm7/B♭ B♭7 1 E♭
once in my life - time I'm going to do great things.
Fm7 B♭7 2 E♭ B♭m7/E♭ E♭6/9
Just things.
f
mf
mp rit.

WHAT KIND OF FOOL AM I?

(From the Musical Production "STOP THE WORLD — I WANT TO GET OFF")

Words and Music by LESLIE BRICUSSE
and ANTHONY NEWLEY

Am7 D7 Gsus G7 Cmaj7
emp- ty heart must dwell. What kind of lips are these
clown am I?
Cmaj7 Dm7(add G) G7 Cmaj7
That lied with ev- 'ry kiss? That whis- pered emp- ty words of
What do I know of life? Why can't I cast a- way the
Gm/Bb A7 Gm7 C7 F6
love that left me a- lone like this? Why can't I fall in love
mask of play and live my life? Why can't I fall in love
Dm7-5 C/E D7 Dm7
like an- y oth- er man
'til I don't give a damn
And may- be then I'll know what
Fm G7 1. C Cmaj7 Am7 Fmaj7 G7 2. C Cmaj7 Am7 Fmaj7 Dm7 Cmaj7
kind of fool I am. What kind of am.

AS LONG AS HE NEEDS ME

(From the Columbia Pictures - Romulus film "OLIVER!")

Words and Music by LIONEL BART

2
Cmaj7
C7
F
G7
C
Me. If you are lone - ly then you will know When some - one
Am
D9
Dm7
Fm
G7
Cmaj7
G11
G13-9
needs you you love them so. I won't be - tray his
Cmaj7
A7-9
Dm7
trust, Tho' peo - ple say I must. I've got to
A7-9
Am7
D9
Dm7
Fm
G7
C
stay true, just As Long As He Needs Me.
f

CONSIDER YOURSELF

(From the Columbia Pictures – Romulus film "OLIVER!")

Words and Music by
LIONEL BART

Gm7 C7 F F7+5 F Bb7 Ab/C
go - ing to get a - long! Con - share! If it should chance to be we should see some
ev - er we've got we No - bod - y tries to be lah - di - dah and

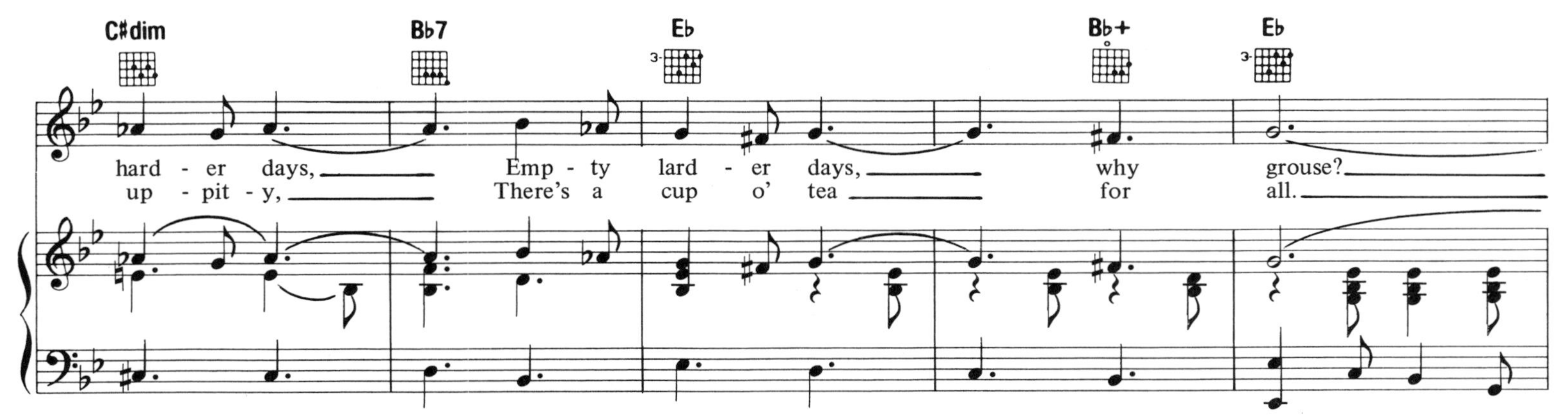
C#dim Bb7 Eb Bb+ Eb
hard - er days, Emp - ty lard - er days, why grouse?
up - pit - y, There's a cup o' tea for all.

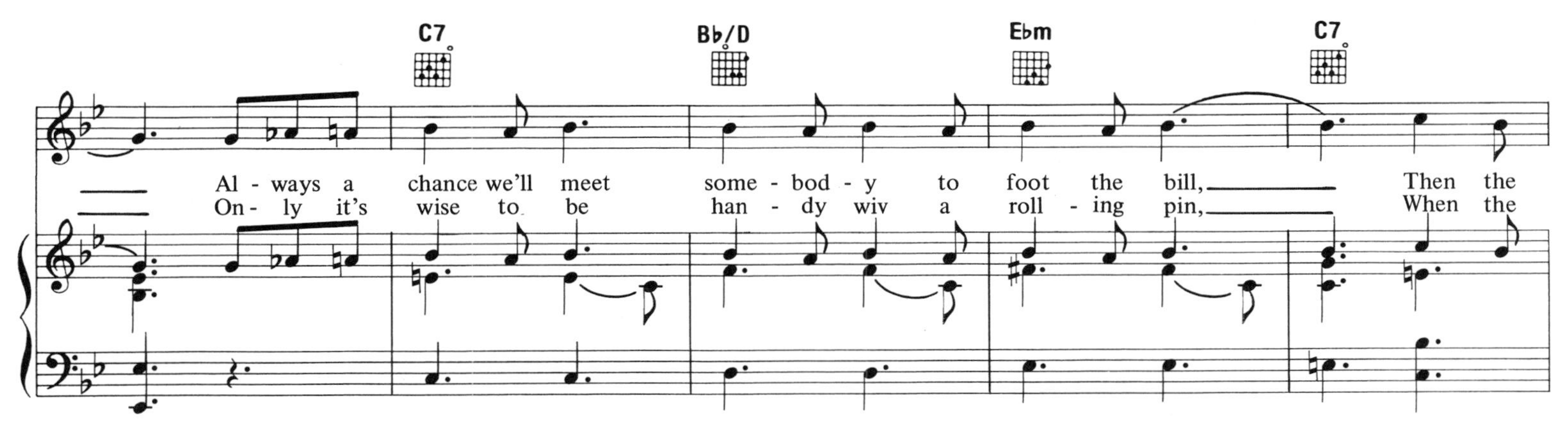
C7 Bb/D Ebm C7
Al - ways a chance we'll meet some - bod - y to foot the bill, Then the
On - ly it's wise to be han - dy wiv a roll - ing pin, When the

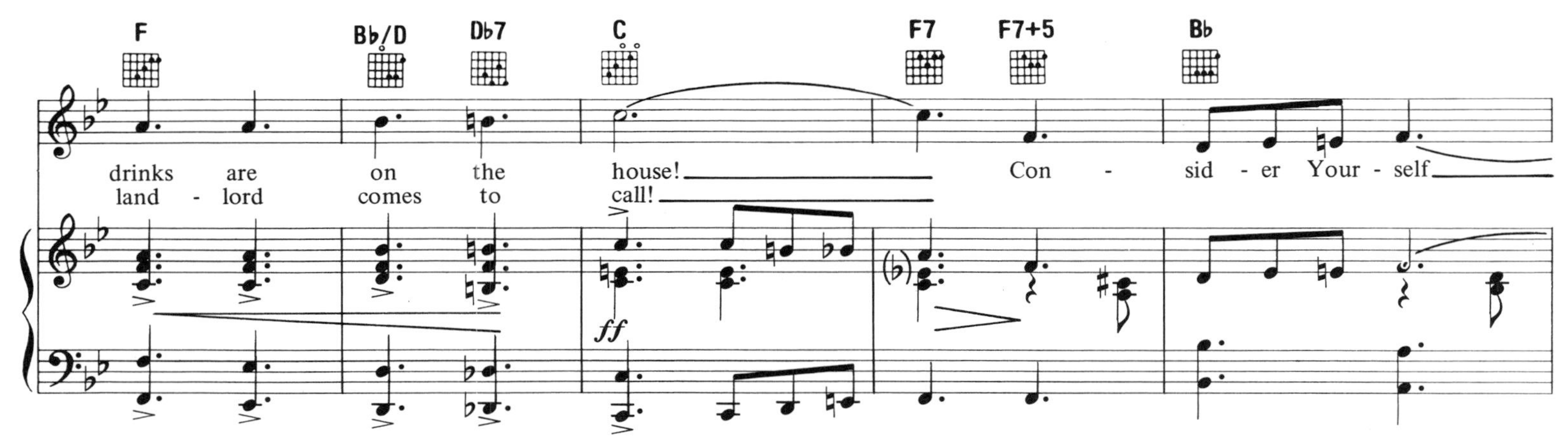
F Bb/D Db7 C F7 F7+5 Bb
drinks are on the house! Con - sid - er Your - self
land - lord comes to call!
ff

G7
Cm
our mate, We don't want to have no
Ab
F7
F7+5
Bb
Fm6/Ab
fuss For aft - er some con - sid - er - a - tion, we can
G7
Cm
Ebm/Gb
1
F7
Bb
Bdim
F7/C
F7+5
state: Con - sid - er Your-self one of us. Con -
2
F7
Bb
one of us.
ff

PEOPLE
(From "FUNNY GIRL")

Words by BOB MERRILL
Music by JULE STYNE

need - ing oth - er child - ren And yet,
Bbm C7 Fmaj7 F6 G Bbm6 Gdim
let - ting our grown up pride
Hide all the need in -
mf
F Fdim Gm7 C7
side, Act - ing more like child - ren, than
E F7 Gm7 F9 Bb
child - ren.
Lov - ers
rit.
mp a tempo

F7
Bb
Cm7
F7
are very special people,
They're the
Eb
Bbmaj7
Fm7
3
luck-i-est people in the world.
3
Bb9
Eb
Ebm
With one person,
One very special
Bb
Fm7
Eb
person,
A feeling deep in your soul

F7 Bb Gm6 Bb6 Gm7

Says: you were half, now you're whole. No more hun-ger and thirst, But

Cm7 F7 Bb Bb7

first, be a per-son who needs peo-ple. Peo-ple who need

mf molto espressivo

Eb Ebm Eb Bb Cm7

peo-ple Are the luck-i-est peo-ple in the

f

1 Bb Gm7 Cm7 F7 | 2 Bb Gm7 Bb6

world. world.

rit. *p*

IF I WERE A RICH MAN

(From the Musical "FIDDLER ON THE ROOF")

Words by SHELDON HARNICK
Music by JERRY BOCK

Cm
D7
G7
To Coda
C
Guitar Tacet
bid - dy, bid - dy rich,
dig - guh, dig - guh, dee - dle dai - dle
man. I'd build a
rall.
Quasi rubato
Fm
Bb7
Ebmaj7
Bbm6
C7
big tall house with rooms by the doz - en, Right in the mid - dle of the town; A
Fm
G7
C
C7
fine tin roof with real wood - en floors be - low. There could be
Fm
Bb7
Ebmaj7
Bbm6
C7
one long stair - case just go - ing up and one e - ven long - er com - ing down; And

Fm F#dim G7 C7

one more lead - ing no - where just for show. I'd fill my

rall.

F G7 C A7

yard with chicks and tur - keys and geese And ducks for the town to see and hear;

Dm7 G7 C C7

Squawk - ing just as nois - i - ly as they can. And each loud

Fm Bb7 Ebmaj7 Bbm6 C7

quack and cluck and gob - ble and honk Will land like a trum - pet on the ear; As

(imitate sounds)

Fm F#dim G7
D.S. al Coda
if to say here lives a wealth - y man.
(Sigh)
rall.
Quasi rubato
CODA
C
Guitar Tacet
Fm Bb7
man. I see my wife, my Gold - e, look-ing like a rich man's
Ebmaj7 Bbm6 C7 Fm G7
wife with a prop-er dou-ble chin;
Su - per - vis - ing meals to her heart's de -
C C7 Fm Bb7
light. I see her put-ting on airs and strut-ting like a pea - cock

Ebmaj7 Bbm6 C7 Fm F#dim

Oy! What a hap-py mood she's in. Scream-ing at the ser-vants day and

G7 C7 Rubato

night. The most im-por-tant men in town will come to fawn on _ me;

3 3 3

Fm Db

They will ask me to ad-vise them, ___ Like Sol-o-mon the wise, "If you

Bbm C7

please, Reb Tev-ye, par-don me, Reb Tev-ye." Pos-ing prob-lems what would cross a rab-bi's eyes.

Freely
Deliberately (in tempo)
Fm7
Bb7
Boi, boi, boi, boi, boi, boi, boi, boi, boi.
And it won't make one bit of dif - f'rence
Ebmaj7
Bbm6
C7
Fm
F#dim
If I an - swer right or wrong?
When you're rich, they think you real - ly
G7
C7
Reflective
F
G7
know.
If I were rich, I'd have the time that I lack, To
rall.
p
C
A7
Dm7
G7
sit in the syn - a - gogue and pray;
And may - be have a seat by the east - ern

C
C7
Fm
Bb7
wall. And I'd dis - cuss the ho - ly books with the learn - ed
Ebmaj7
C7
Fm
F#dim
G7
men sev - en ho - urs ev' - ry day; This would be the sweet - est thing of all.
Tempo I
C
(Sigh) If I were a rich man, Dai - dle, dee - dle, dai - dle, dig - guh, dig - guh, dee - dle, dai - dle,
G7
Cm
D7
dum. All day long I'd bid - dy, bid - dy bum, If I were a wealth - y

G7
C
man. Would-n't have to work hard, Dai-dle, dee-dle, dai-dle dig-guh, dig-guh, dee-dle, dai-dle,
8va
Rubato
G7
Cm
G7
dum. Lord, who made the li-on and the lamb, You de - creed I
8va
Cm
G7
Cm
A7-5
D7-5
G7
should be what I am; Would it spoil some vast e-ter-nal plan, If I were a wealth-y
15ma
8va
C
G7
C
man?
8va
a tempo
8va

MATCHMAKER
(From "FIDDLER ON THE ROOF")

Words by SHELDON HARNICK
Music by JERRY BOCK

Bb
C11
C7
F
C7-9
book And make me a per - fect match.
book And make her a per - fect match.
F
F6
Fmaj7
1,2 Match - mak - er, match - mak - er,
I'll bring the veil,
You know that I'm
You bring the
still ver - y
(M:) Match - mak - er, match - mak - er, We'll bring the veil, You bring the
groom, slen - der and pale;
young, Please take your time;
groom, slen - der and pale;
F
Bring me a ring, for I'm
Up to this min - ute, I
Bring her a ring, for she's
F7
Bb
C11
C7
F
F7sus
F7
long - ing to be the en - vy of all I see. For
mis - un - der - stood that I could be stuck for good. Dear
long - ing to be the en - vy of all she'll see. For

Bbm7
Eb
pop - pa, make him a schol - ar, For
mom - ma, see that he's gen - tle, Re -
me, please, make him a schol - ar, For
Abmaj7
Ab6
To Coda
mom - ma, make him rich as a king. For
mem - ber you were al - so a bride. It's
mom - ma, make him rich as a king. For
Gm7
C7
me, well, I would - n't hol - ler if
her, well, She would - n't hol - ler if
Fm
F7
Bbm
Cm
C7-9
he were as hand - some as an - y - thing.
he were as hand - some as an - y - thing.

F
F6
Fmaj7
Match - mak - er, match - mak - er, make me a match, Find me a
Match - mak - er, match - mak - er, make her a match, Find her a
F
find, catch me a catch; Night af - ter night in the
find, catch her a catch; Night af - ter night in the
F7
Bb
Bbmaj7
C7sus
dark I'm a - lone, So strike me a match of
dark she's a - lone, So find her a match of
C7
F
D.S. al Coda
my own.
her own. (End of Male Lyric)

CODA
Gm7
C7
Fm
not that I'm sen - ti - men - tal. It's
F7
B♭m
Cm
C7-9
just that I'm ter - ri - fied.
8va
F
F6
Fmaj7
Match - mak - er, match - mak - er, plan me no plans, I'm in no
F
rush, May - be I've learned Play - ing with match - es a

F7
Bb
Bbm
girl can get burned. So bring me no ring, Groom me no
(Male:) So bring her a ring, Groom her a
rit.
a tempo
F
G7
groom, Find me no find, Catch me no catch;
groom, Find her a find, Catch her a catch;
C11
C7+5
F
Un - less he's a match - less match!
And make her a match - less match!
8va

SUNRISE, SUNSET

(From the Musical "FIDDLER ON THE ROOF")

Words by SHELDON HARNICK
Music by JERRY BOCK

Moderately Slow Waltz Tempo
(soulful and wistful)

Gm
D7
Gm
G7
beau - ty? When did he grow to be so tall?
fin - ger, Share the sweet wine and break the glass;
Cm
G7
Cm
A7
D
Was - n't it yes - ter - day when they were small?
Soon the full cir - cle will have come to pass.
Gm
D7
Gm
D7
Sun - rise, sun - set, sun - rise, sun - set,
Gm
G7
Cm
F7
Swift - ly flow the days;
Seed - lings turn o - ver - night to

Bbmaj7 Bb6 Am7 D7 Gm

sun - flow'rs, Blos - som - ing e - ven as we gaze.

D7 Gm D7 Gm

Sun - rise sun - set, sun - rise, sun - set, Swift - ly fly the

G7 Cm F7 Bbmaj7 Bb6

years; One sea - son fol - low - ing an - oth - er,

Am7 D7 1 Gm 2 Gm

La - den with hap - pi - ness and tears. tears.

rit.

HELLO, DOLLY!
(From "HELLO, DOLLY!")

Music and Lyric by JERRY HERMAN

Cm
Cm7
F7
Bb6
Bbdim
Dol - ly, you're still glow - in', you're still crow - in', you're still go - in'
F7
Bb
Gm
strong. We feel the room sway - in', for the band's
Fm7
Bb7
Fm7
Bb7
Ebmaj7
Eb6
play - in' one of your old fa - v'rite songs from 'way back when.
Cm6
D7
Gm
Dm
Gm
So take her wrap, fel - las, Find her an emp - ty
gol - ly gee, fel - las, Find her a va - cant

Dm
C9
C9+5
Cm7
F9
lap, fel - las,
knee, fel - las,
Dol - ly 'll nev - er go a - way a -
Bb
Bdim
Cm7
F7
Cm7
F9
gain!
Hel -
go a - way,
C9
C9+5
Cm7
F9
C9
C9+5
Dol - ly 'll nev - er go a - way, Dol - ly 'll nev - er
Cm7
F9
Bb
F7
Bb
go a - way a - gain!

It Only Takes A Moment

Music and Lyric by JERRY HERMAN

Bbmaj7 Gm7 Cm7 F7 Bbmaj7 Gm7 Cm7 F7 Bbmaj7 Bb6
held her
held me
for an in - stant,
But my / his arms felt
Gm G7-9 Cm7 Cm7-5
sure / safe and strong.
It On - ly Takes A
Bb Gm Cm7-5 Bb Gm Cm7 F7 To Coda Bb
Mo - ment, To be loved a whole life long
Bbmaj7 Bb6 Cm7 F7
I've heard it said that love must grow, That to be
mp
Bbmaj7 Bb6 Cm7 F7 Bbmaj7
sure, you must be slow. I saw you smile

Gm7
Cm7-5
and now I know, I'll lis-ten to just my heart, That smile made me
F7+5(b9)
D.S. al Coda
trust my heart. For It
CODA
Bb
long. And that is
mf
Bbmaj7
Bb6
Cm7
F7
Bbmaj7
all that love's a - bout And we'll re - call
Gm7
C9
Cm7-5
Bb
Gm
Cm7-5
when time runs out That it on - ly took a
Bb
Gm
Cm7-5
Bb
Gm
Cm7
F7
Bb
mo - ment To be loved a whole life long.
R.H.
L.H.

Do I Hear A Waltz?

G F# G Eb
I can't hear a waltz, Oh, my Lord, there it goes a - gain!
You must hear a waltz? E - ven stran - gers are danc - ing now:
Am6 D7 G6 G
Why is no - bod - y danc - ing in the street?
An old la - dy is waltz - ing in her flat,
R.H.
A7sus A9 Am7 D7 C6 C#dim F# G
Can't they hear the beat? Ma - gi - cal, mys - ti - cal, mir - a - cle,
Waltz - ing with her cat. Ros - es are danc - ing with pe - o - nies.
mf
D+ G D7sus D7 D+ D7 Gsus9 G C6 C#dim
Can it be? Is it true? Things are im - pos - si - bly
Yes, it's true! Don't you see? Ev - 'ry - thing's sud - den - ly
F# G F#7 G A7sus A7 Am7 D7 G F#
lyr - i - cal. Is it me? No, it's you! I do hear a
Vi - en - nese, Can't be you! Must be me! Do I Hear A
mp

G
Am7
D7
Am7
D7
waltz? I see you and I hear a waltz! It's
Waltz? I want more than to hear a waltz: I
C
Bm
Am6
G
Gdim
Am7
A7
D7
what I've been wait - ing for all my life, To hear a
want you to share it 'cause Oh, boy, Do I Hear A
cresc.
1
G
D7sus
D7
waltz! Do
2
G
C6
G
C6
Waltz?
f
marcato
poco a poco
cresc.
G
C6
G
Cmaj7
G
Cmaj7
G
Cmaj7
G
Cmaj7
G
Am7
I hear a waltz. I hear a
G
Am7
G
Am7
G
Am7
G
Am7
G
waltz.
accel.
ff

HALF A SIXPENCE

Words and Music by
DAVID HENEKER

C7
D
Em7
E♭7
D
A7
lot. But six - pence is the on - ly thing I got.
rall.
F7
B♭
Still half a six - pence is bet - ter than
F7
B♭6
half a pen - ny, is bet - ter than half a far - thing,
Cm7
Bdim
F7
is bet - ter than none. It's a to - ken

Cm
F7
B♭
of our e - ter - nal love. When you're far a -
C7
F9
Dm
A7
F7
Cm7
F+
way, touch it ev - 'ry day. And though that
B♭
F7
half a six - pence can on - ly mean half a ro - mance,
B♭
re - mem - ber that half a ro - mance is bet - ter than

Fm6
G7
Cm
none.
But when I'm with you,
F7
B♭
A♭7
G7
one and one make two
and like - wise
Cm
Bdim7
Cm
F7
1
B♭
two half six - pen - ces join'd to - geth - er make one.
F7
2
B♭
B♭6
one.

ON A CLEAR DAY (YOU CAN SEE FOREVER)

(From "ON A CLEAR DAY YOU CAN SEE FOREVER")

Words by ALAN JAY LERNER
Music by BURTON LANE

Dm7/G
G7
Dm7
G7
star. You feel part of ev- 'ry moun- tain, sea and shore. You can
mf più espr.
Cmaj7
Dm6
A7
D7
Edim
Gmaj7
hear, from far and near, a world you've nev- er heard be- fore. And on a clear day,
G
Bm7
E9
Bm
E9
Am7
G6
Am7
G6
1. Am7
D7
On that clear day You can see for- ev- er and ev- er-
cresc.
G
Em
Am7
D7
2. Am7
G6
Am7
G6
Am7
more! On a ev- er and ev- er and ev-
mp
p poco rit.
D7
G
Em9
Am9
D7
Gmaj7
G
er- more!
mf
accel.
p

WHAT DID I HAVE THAT I DON'T HAVE?

Words by Alan Jay Lerner
Music by Burton Lane

Slowly with expression

F6 G7 C6 Cmaj7 Cdim G9
just a vic - tim of time, Ob - so - lete in my prime!
can I go to re - pair all the wear and the tear;
B7 E7 A7 Fm G7 C C+
Out of date and out - classed by my past.
Till I'm once a - gain the pre - vious me?
What did he love that
What did he like that
mp
C C+ C C6 C♯dim G7 Gdim G7 C7
there's none of?
I'm not like?
What did I lose the sweet warm knack of?
What was the charm that I've run dry of?
Would - n't I be the
What would I give if
F E9 Am D7 A♭7 C Em7
late great me if I knew how?
my old know - how still knew how!
Oh!
What did I have I
mf
f
F G7 1 C B♭ G7 2 C
don't have now?
don't have now?
8va
cresc.
rit.
f
R.H.

Nothing Can Stop Me Now!

By Leslie Bricusse and Anthony Newley

Bbm7 C7+5 Fm7 Bb13
-ised land, I'm gon-na find it and how.
to have, I'm here-by mak-ing a vow.
Eb Gm Bbm6 C7+5 Fm7 Db9
Hope is high and I'm gon-na cling to it, Tie ev-'ry string
From now on I'm gon-na be-gin a-gain, Stick out my chin
F7 Bb7 Eb Eb+
to it, Give ev-'ry-thing to it. I'll make all my
a-gain, Go in and win a-gain. Get you gone, you
Eb6 Eb+ Eb Gm7 C7
dreams come true Be-fore my fi-nal bow.
sky of grey Fare-well you fur-rowed brow.

Ab Ab+ Ab6 Bb9 Gm
How I'll do it, who can say? But I
Now my fu - ture's crys - tal clear. No more
Bb+ Bb Edim Fm7 Db9
know I will some day. Watch out, world, I'm
woe for me to fear. I'm gon - na stand this world up -
C7+5 Fm F7 Bb7 1 Eb Bb13
on my way, Noth - ing Can Stop Me Now.
on its ear, And I'll suc - ceed some
2 Cm Cm(+7) Cm7 Cm6 Fm7 E7-5 Eb
how. Noth - ing Can Stop Me Now.
cresc.
f
sfz

WHO CAN I TURN TO
(When Nobody Needs Me)
(From the Musical Production "THE ROAR OF THE GREASEPAINT - THE SMELL OF THE CROWD")

Words and Music by LESLIE BRICUSSE
and ANTHONY NEWLEY

Fmaj7
F
Em7
Cmaj7/E
Am
Am7
Fmaj7
Dm6
and no - one be - side me, I'll go on my way, and
Em7
A7
Dm
Dm7
G7
af - ter the day, The dark - ness will hide me; And
Cmaj9
C6
Dm7
G7
may - be to - mor - row I'll find what I'm af - ter
Dm7
G7
C
C6
Cmaj7
C
I'll throw off my sor - row, beg steal or bor - row

Gm Gm7 C9 F F+
my share of laugh - ter. With you I could learn to,
Dm6 E7 Am Am(+7) Am7
with you on a new day, But
F C6 Dm7 Db7
who can I turn to if you turn a - way?
1 C6 Dm7/C G13
cresc.
2 C6 Dm7/C G13 Cmaj7 C6
way?
rit. e dim.

A Wonderful Day Like Today

Words and Music by LESLIE BRICUSSE and ANTHONY NEWLEY

Fm7
1. F7
Bbsus
Bb7
won- der- ful day like to- day. On a
won- der- ful morn-
2. F7
Bb7-9
Eb6
tacet
Ab
Ab+
-ing like this. On a morn- ing like this I could
Fm/Ab
Bb7/Ab
Eb/G
Cm7
Bmaj7
Fm7
kiss ev- 'ry- bod- y I'm so full of love and good-
Ebmaj7
Ab
Ab+
will. Let me say fur- ther- more I'd a-
Fm
Bb7
Gm7
Gb+
-dore ev- 'ry- bod- y to come and dine. The plea- sure's mine, And

F7
Fm7/Bb
Eb
Ebmaj7
tacet
I will pay the bill. May I take this oc- ca- sion to say
Eb6
Eb
Fm7
That the whole hu- man race should go down on its knees,
Bb7
F7
Bb7
Gm7
Show that we're grate- ful for morn- ings like these,
C7
Ab6
G7
Cm7
For the world's in a won- der- ful way,
F9
Fm7
Bb7
Eb
On a won- der- ful day like to- day.

CABARET
(From the Musical "CABARET")

Music by JOHN KANDER
Words by FRED EBB

Bb9 | 1 Eb | Fm7 | Bb9 | 2 Eb

cab - a - ret. ___ ret. Come taste the

𝄋 Abm | Eb | Cm | Cm+7

wine, Come hear the band, Come blow the horn, start

Cm7 | F9 | Bb7 | Eb

cel - e - brat - ing, Right this way, your ta - ble's wait - ing. {No use per -
{Start by ad -

Bb9 | Bb9+5 | Eb | Bb7+5 | Eb | Ebmaj7

mit - ting some proph - et of doom _ To wipe ev - 'ry smile a -
mit - ting from cra - dle to tomb ___ is - n't that long a

Bbm7
Eb7
Ab
Adim
To Coda
Gm7
C9
way;
stay;
Life is a cab - a - ret, old chum,
Fm7
Bb11
Eb
D.S. al Coda
Come to the cab - a - ret,
Come taste the
CODA
Gm7
C9
Ab
Adim
Gm7
C9
ret, old chum,
On - ly a cab - a - ret, old chum,
Fm7
Bb11
Eb
Bb9+5 Eb
so come to the cab - a - ret.
sfz
8va

Willkommen
(From the Musical "CABARET")

Words by FRED EBB
Music by JOHN KANDER

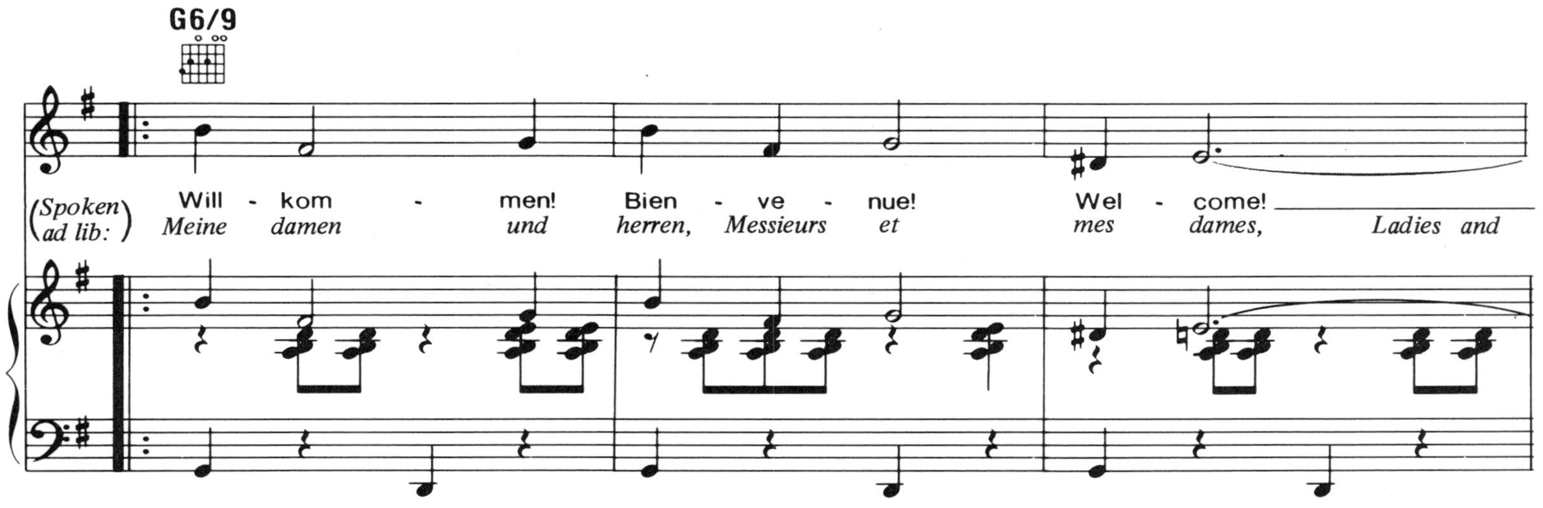

Am7
D11
Am7
D11
Am
Stran - ger,
Glück - lich zu
Good - evening;
Wie gehts?
D7-9
Gmaj7
G6/9
se - hen. Je suis en - chan - té.
Comment sa va? Do you feel good?
A13
Am7
Hap - py to see you, Blei - be, Res - te,
Ich bin euer confrencier, Je suis votre compere, I am your host!
D7
G6/9
Stay,
(Sung) Und sa - ge.
Will - kom - men! Bien - ve - nue!

E7
1
Am7
D7
Wel - come!
Im Cab - a - ret, au Cab - a - ret, to Cab - a -
G
2
Am
ret!
ret,
au Cab - a -
Am9
D13
G
ret, to Cab - a - ret!
8va
sf

IF HE WALKED INTO MY LIFE

(From "MAME")

D7 G9 G9+5 G7 G9 G9+5 Gm7 C9 C9+5 Fmaj7
Was I soft or was I tough? Did I give e - nough? Did I give too much?
Cm6 D7-9 Gm Gm7 B♭m6
At the mo - ment that {he / she} need - ed me, Did I ev - er turn a -
Am7 Fdim Gm7 G9
way? Would I be there when {he / she} called, If {He / She} Walked In - to My
C7sus C7-9 Fmaj9 C7 F6
Guitar Tacet
Life to - day.
Were his days a lit - tle dull?
Did she mind the lone - ly nights?
mf
Fmaj7 F7 Am7 D7 G9 G9+5
Were his nights a lit - tle wild? Did I o - ver - state my
Did she count the emp - ty days? Was I si - lent, was I

G7 G9 G9+5 Gm7 C9 C9+5 Fmaj7

plan? Did I stress the man? And for - get the child.
cold? Was I quick to scold? Was I slow to praise?

A7-5 D7-9 Gm Gm7 Bbm6 Am7

And there must have been a mil - lion things, That my heart for - got to say.

Fdim Gm7 G9 C7sus C7-9 F

Would I think of one or two, If {He/She} Walked In - to My Life to - day.

Guitar Tacet

Db Db6 Dbmaj7 Db6 Ebm7

Should I blame the times I pam - pered {him,/her,} Or blame the times I bossed {him;/her;}

Ab7 Db Db6 Dbmaj7 Db6 Gm7

What a shame I nev - er real - ly found the {boy,/girl,} Be - fore I lost {him./her.}

C7 Fdim F6 Fmaj7 F7 Am7
Were the years a lit - tle fast. Was {his/her} world a lit - tle free?
D7 G9 G9+5 G7 G9 G9+5 Gm7 C9 C9+5 Fmaj7
Was there too much of a crowd? All too lush and loud and not e-nough of me.
Cm6 D7 Gm Gm7 Bbm Am7
Though I'll ask my-self my whole life long, What went wrong a-long the way;
Fdim Gm7 G9 C7sus C7-9 Am7
Would I make the same mis - takes If {He/She} Walked In - to My Life to - day? If that
D7 G9 Bbm6 C7-9 Fmaj7 Ab6 Fmaj7
{boy/girl} with the {bu - gle/prom - ise} walked in - to my life to - day.
rall.

MAME
(From "MAME")

Music and Lyric by
JERRY HERMAN

A9 Dm Dm(+7) Dm7 G7 G9+5
band, The whole plan - ta - tion's hum - min' since
speech, You may be from Man - hat - tan, but
C C#dim Dm7 G7 C C6
you brought Dix - ie back to Dix - ie - land. You make the
Geor - gia nev - er had a sweet - er peach. You make our
Cmaj7 C#dim Dm7 G7 Dm Dm(+7)
cot - ton eas - y to pick, Mame, You give my
black - eyed peas and our grits, Mame, Seem like the
Dm7 G7 E7 Dm6 E7 Am Am(+7)
old mint ju - lep a kick, Mame, You make the
bill of fare at the Ritz, Mame, You came, you

Am7 Adim Em A9
old mag - no - lia tree blos - som at the men - tion of your name,
saw, you con - quered and ab - so - lute - ly noth - ing is the same.
Dm Dm(+7) Dm7 G7 Em Em(+7) Em7
You've made us feel a - live___ a - gain, You've giv - en
Your spe - cial fas - ci - na - tion 'll Prove to be
A9 D7 Dm7 G7 G7-9
us the drive___ a - gain, To make the South re - vive___ a - gain,
in - spi - ra - tion - al, We think you're just sen - sa - tion - al,
1 C Cdim Dm7 G7
Mame.
2 C
Mame.___

WE NEED A LITTLE CHRISTMAS
(From "MAME")

D7
Dm6
E7
deck the halls a-gain now.
on that ev-er-green bough.
Am6
E7
Am
D7
G
Gmaj7
G6
G+
G
For We Need A Lit-tle Christ-mas, Right this ver-y min-ute,
For I've grown a lit-tle lean-er, Grown a lit-tle cold-er,
3. For we need a lit-tle mu-sic, Need a lit-tle laugh-ter,
Am
D7
G
Gmaj7
G6
G7
C
Can-dles in the win-dow, Car-ols at the spin-et. Yes, We Need A Lit-tle
Grown a lit-tle sad-der, Grown a lit-tle old-er. And I need a lit-tle
Need a lit-tle sing-ing Ring-ing through the raft-er. And we need a lit-tle
D7
G
Gmaj7
G6
A7
Christ-mas, Right this ver-y min-ute, It has-n't snowed a sin-gle flur-ry, But
an-gel, Sit-ting on my shoul-der,
snap-py "hap-py ev-er aft-er,"
D7
Am
D9
D7
G
D.S. to 3rd Lyric
San-ta, dear, we're in a hur-ry. 2. So Need A Lit-tle Christ-mas now!
sf

MY CUP RUNNETH OVER
(From "I DO! I DO!")

Words by TOM JONES
Music by HARVEY SCHMIDT

G7
C
Em
Dm
sleep. And some - times I whis - per what I'm think - ing
ly. I mem - or - ize mo - ments that I'm fond - est
Em
Dm7
G11
C
of: My cup run - neth o - ver with luh
of: My cup run - neth o - ver with luh
8va
mf
Am
Dm
G7
C
uh uh uh uh
uh uh uh uh
mf
Am
1 Dm7
G7
2 Dm7
uh uv. Some - uv!
uh

G7
C
Am7
Dm9
In on - ly a mo - ment, we both will be
G7
C
Am
Dm9
old; We won't e - ven no - tice the world turn - ing
G7
C
Em
Dm
cold. And so in this mo - ment with sun - light a -
Em
Dm7
G11
C
3
bove; My cup run - neth o - ver with luh
mf

Am Dm7 G7

uh uh uv, with

C Am Dm7 G7

Luh uv, with

mf *sempre cresc.*

C Am Dm7 G7

Luh uh uv, with

8va

C

lu huh uv!

f *ff* *sf*

THE HAPPY TIME

Music by JOHN KANDER
Words by FRED EBB

G
mem-ber the paint - ed horse, the ca - rou - sel, the choc - 'late kiss, the
mem-ber the com - pli - ment you once re - ceived, the lie you told they
mem-ber the tu - lip trees you walked a - mong, the game was old, the
D7 G F#m7 B7 Em
ca - ra - mel, the hap - py time. Re - mem - ber the pale
all be - lieved, the hap - py time. Re - mem - ber your first
play - er young, the hap - py time. Re - mem - ber a long
Em7 A9 A7 D
pink sky, your first Eas - ter hat. And
school play, the sound of ap - plause. Why
deep sigh, a ten - ta - tive kiss. And
Dm7 G9 C C7/B♭
if you should ask me why the rea - son I ask you this is
do I go on this way? I'm on - ly re - mind - ing you be -
if you should ask me why, the rea - son I ask you that is

A7
D7
1,2
G
E7♯5
Am9
that I want to re-mem-ber you re-mem-ber-ing the hap-
cause I want to re-mem-ber you re-mem-ber-ing the hap-
this: I'm long-ing to
D7
G
Gmaj7
py time.
py time.
8va
G
Gmaj7
G
Gmaj7
G
D7
3
G
Re-mem-ber the see you smile and
Re-mem-ber the

D7
G
hear you laugh so I can have a pho - to-graph, and re-mem - ber
E7♯5
Am9
D7
you re-mem - ber-ing the hap - py
G
Gmaj7
G
Gmaj7
time.
8va
G
Gmaj7
G

ZORBÁ THEME
(Life Is)

(from the Musical Production "ZORBÁ")

Lyrics by
FRED EBB

Music by
JOHN KANDER

A♭
Life is where you wait while you're wait-ing to leave.
E♭m7(A♭ bass)
Life is where you grin and grieve.
F
8va
F
F
Hav-ing if you're luck-y, want-ing if you're not.
F(E bass)
Look-ing for the ru - by un-der-neath the rot.
F7(E♭ bass)
D7
Hun-gry for the pi - laf in

G
Eb7
some-one else-'s pot but that's the on-ly choice you've
Ab
got!
8va
Ab
Life is where you stand just be - fore you are flat.
Ebm7(Ab bass)
Life is on-ly that, Mis-ter, Life is simp-ly that, Mis-ter,

A♭
That and noth-ing more than that.
8va
A♭
Life is what you feel till you
3
can't feel at all.
E♭m7(A♭ bass)
Life is where you fly and
F
fall.

F
Fmaj7
Run-ning for the shel - ter nak-ed in the snow, Learn-ing that a tear drops
F7(E♭ bass)
D9
an - y-where you go. Find-ing it's the mud that makes the ros - es grow. But
G
E♭7
A♭
that's the on - ly choice you know.
8va
gliss.
poco accel.
poco . . . a . . . poco . . . cresc. e accel . . . . .

Ebm7(Ab bass)
Ab Gb Ab Gb
Ab Gb
Wait! Once a-gain.
Moderato(in 4)
Ab
Ab
Life is what you do while you're wait-ing to die.

Rubato
E♭m7(A♭ bass)
This is how the time goes by.
Moderato (in 4)
A♭
p
8va
Presto

BEING ALIVE
(From "COMPANY")

Words and Music by
STEPHEN SONDHEIM

Am7 Fmaj9 Am7/D Dm7/G G13
short and put me through hell and give me sup - port for BE-ING A - LIVE,
Dm7/G Fmaj7/G Dm7/G G13 Dm7/G Fmaj7/G Dm7/G G13
Make me a - live, Make me a - live.
Dm7/G Fmaj7/G Ab/Bb C
Make me con - fused, mock me with praise,
Cdim Ab/Bb Dm7/G G13
Let me be used, Var - y my days,
Dm7/G G7 Dm7/G G13 G9 G9+5 F/G Em
But a - lone is a - lone,
cresc.

F6/G G9 G9+5 Dm7/G G13 Dm7/G G13 C6/9
not a - live. Some-bod - y crowd me with
F C6/9 G7(b9) C6/9
love, Some-bod - y force me to care, Some-bod - y make me come
Am7 Fmaj9 Am7/D Dm7/G G13
through, I'll al-ways be there as fright-ened as you, to help us sur - vive
Fmaj7/G Dm7/G G13 Dm7/G G13 Dm7/G G13
BE - ING A - LIVE, BE - ING A - LIVE,
Dm7/G G13 C Bb/C C Bb/C C Bb/C C9(alt.)
BE-ING A - LIVE.

YOU COULD DRIVE A PERSON CRAZY

(From the Musical Production "COMPANY")

Music and Lyrics by
STEPHEN SONDHEIM

Gm9
C7
doo) First you make a per - son ha - zy
Gm7
Gm7/C
F7
so a per - son could be had. (Doo doo doo doo
F9
F7
B♭6
C/F
doo) Then you leave a per - son dan - gling
B♭6
C/F
F
Dm
sad - ly out - side your door, which it on - ly makes a

Dm7/G
G7
Dm7/G
G7
C7
per - son
glad - ly
want you e - ven more.
no chord
Gm9
C9
I could un - der - stand a per - son
Gm7
Gm7/C
Fmaj9
if it's not a per - son's bag.
(Doo doo doo doo
Am7
D7
doo) I could un - der - stand a per - son

Am7
D7
Gm
if a per - son was a drag. (Doo doo doo doo
B♭6
B♭m7
doo) But worse 'n' that, a per - son that,
F
D9
D7
tit - il - lates a per - son and then leaves her flat is
Dm7/G
G7
Dm7
G7
G9♭5
Dm7
cra - zy, he's a trou - bled per - son,

G7
B♭m
F
C7
he's a tru - ly cra - zy per - son him -
F
Gm7/C
no chord
self! (Doo doo doo doo doo) You could drive a per - son
Gm9
C7
Gm7
Gm7/C
bug - gy, you could blow a per - son's
Fmaj9
cool. (Doo doo doo doo doo) Like you make a per - son

Gm9
C7
Gm7
Gm7/C
hug - gy
while you make her feel a
F7
F9
F7
fool. (Doo doo doo doo doo) When a per - son says that
B♭6
C/F
B♭6
C/F
F
you've up - set her,
that's when you're good.
Dm
Dm7/G
G7
You im-per - son-ate a per - son

Dm7/G
G7
C7
no chord
better than a zombie should, I could understand a
Gm9
C9
Gm7
Gm7/C
person if he wasn't good in
Fmaj9
bed. (Doo doo doo doo doo) I could understand a
Am7
D7
Am7
D7
person if he actually was

Gm
dead. (Doo doo doo doo doo) Ex -
B♭6
B♭m7
clu - sive you, e - lu - sive you, will
F
D9
D7
an - y per - son ev - er get the juice of you? You're
Dm7/G
G7
Dm7
G7
G9♭5
Dm7
cra - zy, you're a love - ly per - son,

G7
B♭m
F
you're a mov - ing, deep - ly mal - ad - just - ed,
D♭7♯5
B♭maj7/C
C7
nev - er to be trust - ed cra - zy per - son your -
F
G7♭5
B♭maj7/C
self! Cra - zy per - son
C7
F
your - self!

DAY BY DAY

(From the Musical "GODSPELL")

Words and Music by STEPHEN SCHWARTZ

Dm
G
1 Cmaj7
Fol - low Thee more near - ly, day by day.
2. Light Rock feeling
Cmaj7
Fmaj7
Gm7/F
day by day.
Day by day,
Fmaj7
Gm7/F
Bbmaj7
Am7
Day by day,
Oh, dear Lord, three
Gmaj7
2nd time, play these 4 measures 4 times
Em
things I pray
to see Thee more

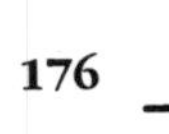

A Em A

clear - ly, love Thee more dear - ly,

Dm G 1.Cmaj7

fol - low Thee more near - ly, Day by day.

2.Cmaj7 Fmaj7

Day by day,

Cmaj7 Fmaj7 Amaj7

Day by day, by day by day by day.

BROADWAY BABY

(From "FOLLIES")

Words and Music by
STEPHEN SONDHEIM

Am Amaj7 Am7 Am6 Am+5Am6 Am7(-5) D7
All twink - ling lights, A spark to pierce the dark from Bat - t'ry Park
a bed and a - chair. Still I'll stick it till I'm on a bill
G7 C C+ C6 Cmaj7 Cmaj9 C
to Wash - ing - ton Heights. Some day may - be,
all o - ver Times Square. Some day may - be,
G11/D G11 G7 To Coda Eb9 D9 Db9 D9 Eb9 E9 F9 G9
All my dreams will be re - paid. Heck, I'd e - ven play the maid to be in a
If I stick it long e - nough,
C Ab7 Db+11 G13 C
show.
F7 C7
Say, Mis - ter pro - duc - er, Some girls get the breaks.

G7
Just give me my cue, sir.
D9 D9sus4 D+11 D9(no3rd) D7 9/6 D9(-6) D9(no3rd) D+11
I've got what it takes.
A7
Say, Mis - ter Pro - duc - er,
B7(-9) B7(+9)/F♯ B7(-9) B7(+9)/F♯
I'm talk - in' to you, sir.
C♯9 D♯9 D9 G-13
I don't need a lot, On - ly what I got, Plus a tube of grease - paint and a fol - low spot! I'm a
Coda
E♭9 D9 D♭9 D9 E♭9 E9 F9 G9 A♭13/9
I can get to strut my stuff,
Work - ing for a nice man like a
D9 G13/9 C
Zieg - feld or a Weiss - man in a big - time Broad - way show!

I DON'T KNOW HOW TO LOVE HIM

(From "JESUS CHRIST SUPERSTAR")

Words by TIM RICE
Music by ANDREW LLOYD WEBBER

Slowly, tenderly and very expressively

Asus A D G D G D
else. I don't know how to take this
G G6 G D/A A D/F# A
I don't see why he moves me He's a man he's just a
D A F#m7 Bm F#m7 Bm
man And I've had so man-y men be-fore In
G D/F# Em D Asus G D/F# D
ver-y man-y ways He's just one more
p

G
F#7
Should I bring him down
should I scream and shout
mp
cresc.
poco
a
poco
Bm
Bm/A
G
D/A
C
Should I speak of love
let my feel - ings out?
I nev - er thought I'd
ff
G
D
G
D/F#
Em
come to this
what's it all a - bout?
f
dim
poco
a
poco
Asus
A
D
G
D
G
D
Don't you think it's rath - er fun - ny
Yet if he said he loved me
mp

G G6 G D/A A D/F♯ A
I should be in this po - si - tion? I'm the one who's al - ways
I'd be lost I'd be fright - ened I could - n't cope just could - n't
D A F♯m7 Bm7 F♯m7 Bm7
been So calm so cool, no lov - er's fool
cope I'd turn my head I'd back a - way I
G D/F♯ Em D Asus G D/F♯ D
Run - ning ev - 'ry show He scares me so
would - n't want to know He scares me
p
D G D/F♯ D G D/F♯ D
so I want him so I love him so
mp
mf

SUPERSTAR
(From "JESUS CHRIST SUPERSTAR")

Lyric by TIM RICE
Music by ANDREW LLOYD WEBBER

C7
Eb
If you'd come to - day you would have reached a whole na - tion
Did you mean to die like that? Was that a mis - take ___ or
F7
C7 Gm7 C7
(Choir)
C
(Don't you get me
Is - rael in 4 B C had no mass com - mu - ni - ca - tion
Did you know your mess - y death would be a re - cord break - er?
C
wrong)
(Don't you get me
F7
wrong now)
(Don't you get me
Don't you get me wrong ___
Don't you get me wrong ___
F7
wrong)
(Don't you get me
C
wrong now)
(I on - ly want to
Don't you get me wrong ___
Don't you get me wrong ___

C7
know)
(I on-ly want to
F7
know now)
(I on-ly want to
On-ly want to know
On-ly want to know
F7
know)
(I on-ly want to
C7
know now)
(Choir)
C
On-ly want to know
On-ly want to know
Je - sus Christ
F
Bb
F
C
Je - sus Christ Who are you? What have you sac - ri - ficed?
Je - sus Christ
F
Bb
F
C
Je - sus Christ Who are you? What have you sac - ri - ficed?
Je - sus Christ

F
Bb
F
C
Su - per-star
Do you think you're what they say you are?
Je - sus Christ
F
Bb
F
1. C
C Eb F F#dim C
Su - per-star
Do you think you're what they say you are?
C Eb F F#dim C
Eb F F#dim C
C (Tacet)
2. C
say you are?
C
F
Bb
F
C
(Repeat and Fade)
Je - sus Christ
Su - per-star
Do you think you're what they say you are?

WHO IS SILVIA?

Words by WILLIAM SHAKESPEARE
Music by GALT MacDERMOT

Am6
B7
Em
Em
she might ad - mired ___ be. Is
be - ing helped, in - hab-its there. Then to Sil - via let
F#7
B7
Em
A7
D7
us sing. That Sil-via is ex - cel - ing;
G
Bm
G
Bm
G
Bm
she ex - cels each mor - tal thing up - on the dull earth
C
Am6
B7
Em
dwell - ing; to her let us gar - lands bring. ___
rit.
pp

Broadway Musicals

Show by Show

Broadway Musicals Show By Show 1891 - 1916
33 classics from shows such as: *Robin Hood, Florodora, Babes In Toyland, The Merry Widow,* and more. Songs include: After The Ball • The Bowery • Give My Regards To Broadway • I Love You So! (The Merry Widow Waltz) • The Isle Of Our Dreams • Kiss Me Again • March Of The Toys • Mary's A Grand Old Name • My Hero • Simple Melody • Streets Of New York • Toyland • and more.
00311514 $12.95

Broadway Musicals Show By Show 1917 - 1929
Over 40 songs from the era's most popular shows, including: *Ziegfeld Follies, The Student Prince In Heidelberg, No No Nanette, Oh, Kay!, Show Boat, Fifty Million Frenchmen,* and more. Songs include: The Birth Of The Blues • Can't Help Lovin' Dat Man • Fascinating Rhythm • How Long Has This Been Going On? • I'm Just Wild About Harry • Ol' Man River • A Pretty Girl Is Like A Melody • St. Louis Blues • Second Hand Rose • Tea For Two • You Do Something To Me • You're The Cream In My Coffee • and more.
00311515 $14.95

Broadway Musicals Show By Show 1930 - 1939
A collection of over 45 songs from the decade's biggest Broadway hits, including: *Anything Goes, Porgy And Bess, Babes In Arms, On Your Toes* and more. Songs include: Begin The Beguine • Embraceable You • Falling In Love With Love • Friendship • I Get A Kick Out Of You • I Got Rhythm • The Lady Is A Tramp • My Funny Valentine • My Heart Belongs To Daddy • On Your Toes • Smoke Gets In Your Eyes • Strike Up The Band • Summertime • It Ain't Necessarily So • and more.
00311516 $14.95

This unique series explores Broadway's biggest hits year by year and show by show. Interesting facts and trivia as well as arrangements for the best songs from each show are presented in a package no Broadway fan can resist! The text about the shows was written by renowned Broadway historian Stanley Green, and is drawn from his book *Broadway Musicals Show By Show.* This is definitely the ultimate collection of Broadway music and history — be sure to collect the whole series!

Broadway Musicals Show By Show 1940 - 1949
Show descriptions and over 45 songs from the Broadway hits *Pal Joey, Oklahoma!, Carousel, Annie Get Your Gun, Finian's Rainbow, South Pacific* and more. Songs include: Another Op'nin, Another Show • Bali Hai • Bewitched • Diamond's Are A Girl's Best Friend • If I Loved You • New York, New York • Oh, What A Beautiful Mornin' • Old Devil Moon • Some Enchanted Evening • The Surrey With The Fringe On Top • You'll Never Walk Alone • more.
00311517 $14.95

Broadway Musicals Show By Show 1950 - 1959
55 songs from such classics as *The King And I, My Fair Lady, West Side Story, Gypsy, The Sound Of Music,* and more. Songs include: Do-Re-Mi • Edelweiss • Everything's Coming Up Roses • Getting To Know You • I Could Have Danced All Night • I've Grown Accustomed To Her Face • Let Me Entertain You • Luck Be A Lady • Mack The Knife • Maria • Seventy Six Trombones • Shall We Dance? • Somewhere • Wouldn't It Be Loverly • and more.
00311518 $14.95

Broadway Musicals Show By Show 1960 - 1971
Over 45 songs from shows such as *Oliver!, Cabaret, Camelot, Hello, Dolly!, Fiddler On The Roof, Jesus Christ Superstar, Mame,* and more. Songs include: As Long As He Needs Me • Consider Yourself • Day By Day • I Don't Know How To Love Him • If Ever I Would Leave You • If I Were A Rich Man • People • Sunrise, Sunset • Try To Remember • We Need A Little Christmas • What Kind Of Fool Am I? • and more.
00311521 $14.95

Broadway Musicals Show By Show 1972 - 1988
Over 30 songs from the era of big productions like *Phantom Of The Opera, Evita, La Cage Aux Folles, Les Miserables, Me And My Girl, A Chorus Line, Cats* and more. Songs include: All I Ask Of You • Don't Cry For Me Argentina • I Am What I Am • I Dreamed A Dream • The Lambeth Walk • Memory • The Music Of The Night • On My Own • Send In The Clowns • Tomorrow • What I Did For Love • and more.
00311519 $14.95

Prices, contents and availability subject to change without notice.